Organizing U.S. Foreign Aid

GLOBAL ECONOMY AND DEVELOPMENT CENTER

Launched in 2004, the Global Economy and Development (GED) Center at the Brookings Institution provides a critical forum for research and dialogue on globalization's defining issues. Unique among research programs in this area, GED pulls together scholars across the disciplines of international economics, governance, international relations, development, law, and environmental science to address the complex and interrelated issues surrounding globalization. In each area, GED has a singular goal: to advance compelling, analytically strong recommendations that will materially shape the policy debate. GED draws on the core strengths of the Brookings Institution: disciplinary depth tempered by practical expertise; breadth of inquiry; proven communications capability and convening power; and a reputation for groundbreaking independent research. The program benefits from generous support from Richard C. Blum of Blum Capital Partners and the William and Flora Hewlett Foundation.

Global Economy and Development: Monograph Series on Globalization

Organizing U.S. Foreign Aid

Confronting the Challenges of the Twenty-first Century

Carol Lancaster and Ann Van Dusen

BROOKINGS INSTITUTION PRESS
Washington, D.C.

Copyright © 2005
THE BROOKINGS INSTITUTION
1775 Massachusetts Avenue, N.W., Washington, D.C. 20036
www.brookings.edu

Library of Congress Cataloging-in-Publication data

Lancaster, Carol.
Organizing U.S. foreign aid : confronting the challenges of the twenty-first century /
Carol Lancaster and Ann Van Dusen.
   p.   cm.
Summary: "Recommends fundamental reorganization of U.S. foreign aid, currently
based on outsourcing and management for results, in favor of a more unified approach
emphasizing development education, stringent evaluation, and a new approach to
contracting"—Provided by publisher.
   Includes bibliographical references and index.
   ISBN-13: 978-0-8157-5113-7 (isbn-13, paper : alk. paper)
   ISBN-10: 0-8157-5113-3 (isbn-10, paper : alk. paper)
   1. Economic assistance, American.   I. Van Dusen, Ann.   II. Title.
HC60.L296 2005
338.91'73—dc22
                                             2005012193

9 8 7 6 5 4 3 2 1

The paper used in this publication meets minimum requirements of the
American National Standard for Information Sciences—Permanence of Paper
for Printed Library Materials: ANSI Z39.48-1992.

Typeset in Sabon

Composition by R. Lynn Rivenbark
Macon, Georgia

Printed by Victor Graphics
Baltimore, Maryland

Contents

Figures

Boxes

Foreword

With a reinvigorated administration starting to define its priorities, the time is ripe to shape the debate over U.S. foreign assistance. The recent tsunami tragedy in the Indian Ocean, the war on terrorism, and instability in the Middle East have created an environment where the nation's leaders are willing to consider afresh the organizational framework and strategic purpose of U.S. foreign aid. And the need for such reform is obvious: a recent Brookings study counted more than fifty stated objectives for foreign assistance, and the daunting multiplicity of foreign aid objectives is further complicated by a plethora of U.S. entities involved in the allocation of aid, often with overlapping jurisdictions. Without clear leadership and strategic planning, U.S. foreign assistance risks undergoing a transformation by default rather than design.

Carol Lancaster and Ann Van Dusen tackle the topic of foreign aid reform with analytical vigor in their latest work and provide guidance on the decisive foreign aid choices facing U.S. policymakers. This monograph is part of the Brookings Global Economy and Development (GED) Center's agenda on foreign aid transformation, which also includes the release of *The Other War: Global Poverty and the Millennium Challenge Account* last year. GED is also working in partnership with the Center for Strategic and International Studies on the Foreign Assistance for the 21st Century Project, which will provide concrete recommendations and actionable strategies to forge greater coherence and effectiveness in foreign aid, reflecting advice from seasoned policymakers, NGO representatives, and congressional advisers.

In this monograph, Lancaster and Van Dusen lay out a compelling case that the organizational landscape of foreign aid is hopelessly fragmented. There are two major aid agencies—USAID and the Millennium Challenge Account (MCA)—three smaller aid agencies, and other aid programs or responsibilities in the Department of State, the Department of the Treasury, and almost every other cabinet-level agency. Further, policymaking decisions and program responsibilities are often located in different agencies. This bureaucratic proliferation causes a legion of problems: waste through duplication of effort; high transactions costs, and, most important, a lack of coordination, both internally within U.S. aid programs and externally among U.S. aid-giving programs, their partners overseas, and their recipients.

There are useful procedural lessons to learn from other Western aid-giving countries, although many of them benefit from a parliamentary system that produces a less acrimonious atmosphere surrounding debates over aid-giving form and function. Lancaster and Van Dusen review Britain's successful overhaul of its aid-giving programs in the 1990s, creating the widely acclaimed DFID, as well as lessons from other aid-giving nations such as Denmark and Japan.

Yet any reform attempt, despite being informed by lessons from our partners, must be tailored to our own unique situation, in both its form and its purpose. Today, USAID accomplishes much of its work by increased outsourcing of larger contracts and grants, creating a "wholesaler of wholesalers" system. It has also developed more elaborate control-oriented planning and results-measurement systems. These changes are troubling; for example, they focus more on counting than on doing. These developments also interfere with the simple imperative of getting maximum resources out to the field as quickly as possible.

Lancaster and Van Dusen suggest that the best choice is to unify all aid programs into a single aid agency with unambiguous leadership, and that the second best option is to unify all major aid agencies—at the very least, USAID and the MCA. Whatever the location and specifics of the United States' new approach to foreign assistance, its organizational design will have to allow for greater flexibility in responding to global events, as the catastrophic events of the tsunami recently reminded us. Foreign aid reform must also include a stronger and more appropriate evaluation process, greater emphasis on recipient responsibility, a new approach to contracting and reporting, and a more effective relationship between the field and headquarters. Finally, U.S. foreign assistance agencies need—and deserve—a better relationship with legislators. Across all of these issues, finding the most useful lever for change should be an urgent mission for the U.S. development community in the months and years ahead.

We extend sincere thanks to Richard Blum and the William and Flora Hewlett Foundation for their generous support of our work here at Brookings.

LAEL BRAINARD
Vice President, Global Economy and Development Center
Brookings Institution

Organizing U.S. Foreign Aid

A New Urgency:
International Development and
U.S. Foreign Policy

In September 2002 the White House published a new National Security Strategy for the United States. It was the first fundamental restatement of American foreign policy since the end of the cold war and highlighted three major U.S. goals in the world: defense (especially against terrorism), diplomacy, and development. Earlier that year, the president had announced the creation of the Millennium Challenge Account (MCA), with proposed funding of $5 billion per year, representing a major increase in U.S. aid for international development. The MCA was to be administered through a new independent agency, the Millennium Challenge Corporation. Then, in January 2003, President Bush proposed an additional boost in assistance to fight HIV/AIDS totaling $10 billion, to be spread over five years. The administration's fiscal 2006 budget request includes an increase of 15 percent in the foreign operations account—the fourth consecutive year that the president has sought a significant boost in the international affairs budget. All these proposals have given a prominence to promoting development and improving lives and livelihoods abroad not seen since the early years of the Kennedy administration.

There is, in fact, good reason to elevate development as a major focus of U.S. foreign policy. Many of the most important challenges and opportunities confronting the United States today and in the future emanate from the more than one hundred countries in Asia, Latin America, Africa, the Middle East, and parts of the former Soviet

1

Union—referred to as the "developing world"—where problems of poverty, limited infrastructure, poor education and health services, frequently slow and sometimes volatile rates of economic growth, low levels of investment and high unemployment rates, and, in a number of cases, ethnic, religious, class, and regional cleavages and weak and corrupt governments remain significant. Such conditions can breed terrorism, provide sanctuary for drug and criminal networks, encourage the spread of infectious diseases, and lead to civil conflict, with enormous human suffering and displacement that can spread beyond borders and have a destabilizing effect regionally and even globally.

At the same time, these same developing countries offer many vital opportunities for enhancing the well-being of the United States—through increased trade with and investment in those nations, which can serve as important sources of food, energy, raw materials, medicines, and ideas. China, with its extraordinary economic dynamism, has showed how important rapidly developing countries can become to the United States. India appears to be close behind in the scope of its market and rapidity of its economic progress. The countries of sub-Saharan Africa, with their rich mineral and oil reserves and a population projected to reach over one billion by 2025, have the potential to become a source of economic dynamism if they can get their economic and political houses in order.

The terrorist attack of 9/11 brought the importance of the developing world into focus for the United States in a way never before seen. Americans had a tendency, especially after the end of the cold war, to think that problems in distant countries were of little relevance to their well-being and could be ignored. The events of 9/11 underlined the vulnerabilities of the American homeland and served as a wake-up call to the American public and its political leaders that pervasive poverty, disenfranchisement, and disaffection abroad can have consequences for the United States. President Bush observed, "Poverty does not make poor people into terrorists and murderers. Yet poverty, weak institutions, and corruption can make weak states vulnerable to terrorist networks and drug cartels within their borders."[1]

International development is increasingly a focus of U.S. foreign policy. This shift is a result of emerging international realities and reflects the changing attitudes toward international engagement of American citizens and their political leaders. Public opinion polls, even before 9/11, found growing support among the American public for development aid (even as the public greatly overestimated the size of aid actually provided).[2] Charitable private giving to nongovernmental organizations (NGOs) to further development abroad more than doubled between 1999 and 2003.[3] Foundation giving for international purposes doubled between 1998 and 2002, rising faster than overall giving by a significant amount, with most of this aid provided to developing countries.[4] Corporate giving and engagement in developing countries appear to be expanding as well. Finally, the outpouring of private giving and public support for generous government relief aid in the wake of the tsunami disaster in Asia was extraordinary. We are observing not only an increase in public awareness of economic and social development needs of poor countries, but also an increased engagement in development by a variety of new actors—individuals, corporate enterprises, foundations, NGOs, and religious organizations. Evangelicals and others from the "Christian right" have become increasingly involved and outspoken in support of U.S. government policies and programs to improve the welfare of the poor and disadvantaged abroad, including those for HIV/AIDS victims and, most recently, for environmental protection. All these groups and individuals provide a much expanded constituency supporting the federal government's efforts to push forward international development.

How well is the U.S. government organized today to pursue international development—whether through foreign aid, trade and investment, or debt policies—as a high priority in its foreign policy? Unfortunately, at present, no single entity in the government has the requisite expertise or wields the necessary clout to provide programmatic leadership and policy direction in promoting the United States' international development agenda. Even with the principal tool for promoting development today—foreign aid—the diffusion of such programs across the government and the complex and cumbersome way aid is programmed make it difficult for the administration to deploy this tool effectively to address development issues. Organization and processes are truly, in the old bureaucratic cliché, "where the rubber meets the road." They are also the focus of this book.

This study primarily discusses the organization and management of U.S. foreign aid for development and associated purposes. It examines the missions and purposes of foreign aid—the way it is organized within the federal government and the structure and processes of aid giving itself. It addresses the political context of aid in the United States and abroad, including domestic politics; the way other governments have organized their aid; and the emerging environment of aid giving in the twenty-first century. And it concludes with a discussion of issues and options available to the federal government so that its aid effort can better address the challenges ahead.

The Nature of Development

Surely one of the reasons there have been so many debates about development and foreign aid is that these terms mean different things to different people. "Development," when applied to societies and countries, has usually included the idea of sustained improvement in the human condition and the changes required to bring about that improvement. In the early decades after World War II, when promoting development in poor countries became part of the U.S. foreign policy agenda, the term "development" was used primarily to refer to *economic* development. Progress was measured by the rate of economic growth and the level and growth in annual per capita incomes. In later decades, the idea of development was extended to include social progress—improvements in quality of life indicators such as life expectancy, literacy, and child mortality. In the 1990s the term "sustainable development" was used to refer to economic and social progress that also preserved the environment and that would continue after donor funding had ended. Also during the 1990s, "development" was increasingly used to encompass democracy, empowerment of the poor, and political freedom. At the end of the decade, Amartya Sen defined "development as freedom"—the ability of individuals to choose fulfilling lives (thus encompassing all the previous definitions and more).[5]

Asked how they would define development today, most policy-makers and practitioners would probably emphasize three things: increases in per capita incomes that lead to a sustained reduction in poverty; an expansion in the physical infrastructure and public services (such as education and health) that are both the means and ends of social and economic progress; and increasingly capable and effective governments that provide for security, the rule of law, responsible economic management, social inclusion, and political freedoms that are also means as well as the ends to improving the human condition.

How do countries move from being "developing" to "developed"? Development requires investments in increased production or productivity or both. Investments in turn require productive opportunities, adequate infrastructure, a trained and healthy labor force, and an economic climate supportive of investors (including physical security, the rule of law, the protection of property rights, a reasonable regulatory regime, and a relatively clean and competent government). In order for development to reduce poverty, the poor must have access to services (such as education and health) and assets (for example, land or credit) that enable them to participate in and benefit from economic growth. While foreign aid can provide needed resources, advice, and incentives for reforms, improved growth depends primarily on actions taken by the developing country and its population. Bringing together the necessary components for successful development remains a complex and challenging task, requiring technical expertise (for example, how to strengthen health systems, deliver immunizations in isolated areas, create sustainable microenterprise-lending programs, reform banking systems), knowledge of local conditions, and, last, but not least, political savvy.

What Is Foreign Aid?

The principal tool for promoting development abroad has long been foreign aid. "Foreign aid" (used interchangeably here with "international assistance") is another term that means different things to different people. Some think of it as a policy. Others regard it as any public resource transferred abroad. Still others define it as only those resource transfers that are specifically intended to help recipients. International assistance is not a policy; rather it is an instrument of policy. It has multiple purposes, only one of which is to benefit the recipients of that aid, and it has a specific set of characteristics. International assistance, or foreign aid, as defined here means

> A voluntary transfer of public resources from one government to another government, international organization, or nongovernmental organization (including not-for-profit organizations working on specific issues, public interest organizations, churches and their associated organizations, universities, foundations, even private, for-profit business enterprises) to improve the lives and livelihoods in the country receiving the aid, among other goals.

This definition is close to the definition of official development assistance (ODA) offered by the Development Assistance Committee (DAC) but differs in two ways.[6] First, it defines impact more broadly by including activities intended primarily to address global issues such as HIV/AIDS and global climate change, democracy promotion, and support for economic and social transitions in former socialist countries. Second, our definition is more expansive in what it includes. The DAC defines ODA as those concessional resources transferred to poor countries. Transfers to countries on the World Bank's list of "high income" countries (with per capita incomes above $9,200 in 2001) for three years or more are not considered official development assistance, but rather official assistance (OA). Thus the DAC would not include aid to countries such as Israel, Russia, Ukraine, the Baltic countries, Poland, and Romania in its definition of ODA. Because the DAC's distinction between ODA and OA underestimates the full development assistance effort of the United States, this study includes both OA and ODA in its examination of U.S. international assistance. Funding for cultural exchanges, covert intelligence action, export promotion, the purchase of military equipment, and training or peacekeeping missions will not be counted as international assistance.

Aid can be provided as cash grants, concessional loans, debt cancellation or relief, or in the form of commodities such as food or medicine. It can fund discrete projects, such as road construction; it can be used to finance research, technical assistance and training for individuals in recipient countries; or it can be provided as an incentive for recipients to adopt policies favored by the donor. In this last case, aid is often provided as "non-project assistance," in the form of budget or balance-of-payments support.

In 2003 the United States provided more than $16 billion in international assistance. Total aid worldwide (net of repayments) amounted to approximately $88 billion.[7] Since 1946 the United States has provided nearly $350 billion in international assistance, making it the largest single source of international assistance over the past half century. At the same time, the United States has long been the smallest donor relative to the size of its economy, as figures 1 and 2 show.[8]

The Mission and Purposes of U.S. Foreign Aid

People often complain that the mission of American foreign aid is unclear. In fact, the missions of public policies and programs are often unclear because they tend to be so general. For example, the closest

FIGURE 1. *U.S. Financial Aid—Official Development Assistance and Official Assistance, 1946–2003*

Billions of dollars

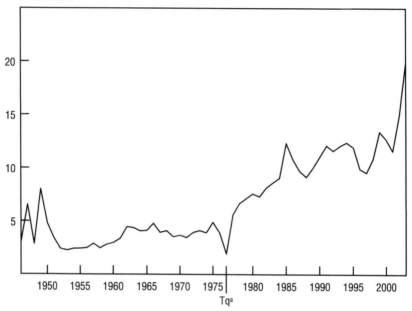

Sources: U.S. Agency for International Development (Greenbook and USAID website, Budget and Policy [www.usaid.gov/policy/budget/]).
a. TQ = transition quarter when the federal government changed its fiscal year.

thing to a statement of mission on the U.S. Agency for International Development website is the following:

> The U.S. Agency for International Development (USAID) is an independent agency that provides economic, development, and humanitarian assistance around the world in support of the foreign policy goals of the United States.

On the other hand, the Department of State's mission is to

> Create a more secure, democratic, and prosperous world for the benefit of the American people and the international community.

FIGURE 2. *DAC-OECD Financial Aid—Official Development Assistance as Percentage of Gross National Income, 2004*

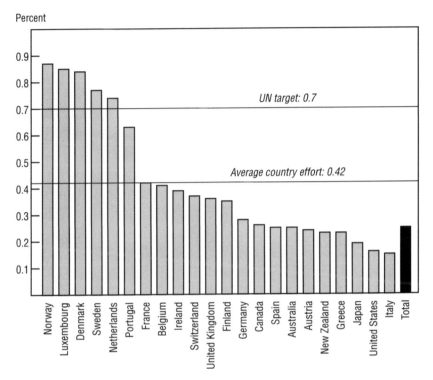

Percent

UN target: 0.7

Average country effort: 0.42

Source: OECD, April 11, 2005.

Neither of these statements provides much enlightenment, especially with regard to the mission of foreign aid. For that, we need to look at how aid is given, to whom, and for what purposes. We need to take into account what donor governments say they are trying to do as well as what they actually do with their aid. Aid for better-off countries or for countries with extremely corrupt or incompetent governments is likely to be for purposes other than development. Aid to poor countries with little geostrategic value to the donor government is likely to be for development or humanitarian purposes. In many cases, a mix of motives drives aid giving.

A Short History of Aid

U.S. foreign aid has always been a multipurposed instrument. Foreign aid as we know it today began in 1947 as a tool of early cold war diplomacy to stabilize the governments and economies of Greece and Turkey in the face of communist pressures at home and abroad. Foreign aid gained prominence soon thereafter in the four-year, $13 billion Marshall Plan for Western Europe—motivated by both humanitarian and diplomatic concerns—to rehabilitate Europe after the war and prevent a slow recovery, especially in France and Italy, from leading to communist electoral victories. The Marshall Plan also sought to encourage Europeans to collaborate on important economic policy questions, helping to create the foundation for what was to become the European Union. Some also saw the Marshall Plan as motivated by U.S. commercial goals—to expand markets for U.S. exports in Western Europe.

With decolonization and the spread of cold war competition to developing countries in Asia, the Middle East, Latin America, and Africa in the late 1950s and early 1960s, foreign aid was seen as a tool to reduce discontent generated by poverty and the consequent temptations of communism by spurring economic progress in these regions and addressing the social and political tensions created by rapid economic change. In 1961 USAID was created by merging several separate aid programs with the primary mission of furthering international development as well as U.S. diplomatic goals. Special efforts were made in Latin America (under the Alliance for Progress), and significant amounts of aid were also provided to Vietnam, Cambodia, and Laos to stabilize those economies during the war in Indochina. U.S. contributions to the World Bank and other multilateral aid agencies increased in the early 1970s, reflecting not only the increasing international focus on development goals, but also the expectation that the United States would lead in both multilateral and bilateral forums.

During this decade, U.S. aid also became an instrument of peace making, especially in the Middle East where economic assistance to Egypt and Israel served as an incentive to maintain a ceasefire and work toward peace. Later, American aid was mobilized during the 1980s to promote political stabilization and development in Central American countries supportive of U.S. policies that challenged the Sandinista government in Nicaragua and assisted the government in El Salvador in its guerilla war.

The methods used to deliver aid, whether to foster development or support diplomacy, also evolved. In the 1960s America financed balance-of-payments and government budgetary gaps and made investments in infrastructure, education, and health. In the 1970s the United States funded projects intended to meet the basic human needs of the poorest in developing countries (for example, primary health care and education, shelter, clean water and sanitation, and agricultural services) and in the 1980s promoted growth through economic policy reforms and investments in private sector development.

In short, while the means may have changed, the goals of U.S. aid for the past forty or more years have been principally to further diplomatic goals, related both to the cold war and peace making in the Middle East, and to further economic and social development in poor countries. In addition, this assistance has traditionally provided food aid and other humanitarian relief during natural disasters such as the several severe droughts in the Sahel and the Horn of Africa during the mid-1970s and mid-1980s or manmade catastrophes such as the Biafra War in Nigeria of the late 1970s or the decades-long civil war in the Sudan.

The end of the cold war did not so much remove foreign policy exigencies as a principal focus of aid-giving as shift the direction of foreign policy concerns. After 1991 promoting economic and social transitions in former socialist bloc countries quickly gained prominence. The intensification of global integration helped raise concerns about the international transmission of disease. In the United States, fears that environmental degradation abroad would affect health and quality of life around the world and in this country led to an increased emphasis on addressing transnational issues through aid. The spread of democracy in developing countries during the 1990s—especially in sub-Saharan Africa and Latin America—gave rise to the use of aid to promote democratic institutions. The many civil conflicts that persisted in Africa and elsewhere and caused so much death, destruction, and displacement prompted the use of aid not just to provide relief but to support postconflict transitions. Finally, aid has gained prominence in recent years as a means to strengthen fragile states and prevent their collapse in the wake of conflict, thus denying sanctuary for terrorists.

What do all these important foreign policy and national security issues have in common? In all cases, the use of diplomacy alone could not bring about the necessary changes sought by the United States. Foreign aid, focused on development institutions and development processes, became a major tool to pursue these important national objectives. For example, working to prevent the international transmission of infectious diseases such as HIV/AIDS inevitably involves efforts to strengthen the health systems of the countries that are struggling with these epidemics. Promoting democracy—seen as both an end in itself and a means of spurring development—typically involves technical assistance to encourage political reforms and strengthen civil society. In postconflict transitions, state institutions must be rebuilt and services provided, along with job creation and community development.

The traditional diplomatic uses of U.S. aid—to reward friends, to provide incentives (or payment) for desired actions, to fortify alliances—have diminished but far from disappeared since the end of the cold war. Indeed, the U.S. "war on terror" has undoubtedly heightened the importance of diplomatically driven aid. And while economic assistance for Israel and Egypt is estimated to decrease to under $800 million in 2005, according to an agreed schedule that would phase out economic assistance to Israel and cut aid to Egypt by half, aid to Pakistan ($380 million), Uzbekistan, Kyrgyzstan, Tajikistan, and Kazakhstan (around $30 million each)—all diplomatic allies in efforts to expel the Taliban government from Afghanistan and destroy al Qaeda—has risen significantly since 2001.[9] Significant progress in a settlement between Israel and the Palestinians would undoubtedly be accompanied by increased financial assistance from the United States, as would a breakthrough in eliminating weapons of mass destruction in North Korea. U.S. diplomatic initiatives in other regions—unforeseen at present but inevitable in an ever-changing world—will necessarily draw on aid for their effectiveness.

What is absolutely clear is that foreign aid is not optional for the United States. Its purposes are central to U.S. interests, values, and well-being. Foreign aid is a critical policy instrument for U.S. engagement in Africa, Asia, the Middle East, Latin America, many countries of Eastern Europe, and nearly all of the former Soviet Union states. The economic, political, and social issues in developing and transition countries, where well over 80 percent of the world's population lives, are now among the most critical foreign policy and national security challenges facing this nation. Scarce aid resources must be deployed for maximum impact, not just to support the interests of the United States and the welfare of the recipients, but also to bolster the American public's support for and understanding of this important policy tool. In short, foreign aid will remain an essential element of U.S. diplomacy. How we organize and manage that aid is a key to its effectiveness.

Organizational Landscape of U.S. Foreign Aid

U.S. international assistance is highly fragmented in terms of both the location of aid programs as well as responsibilities for policy and implementation. The accompanying box lists these various aid programs under the administering agency with actual budget levels for 2004.

U.S. Foreign Aid Programs, 2004

Millions of dollars

Department of State	
Refugee	756
International organizations and programs	320
ESF (policy)	3,263
NIS (distribution)	584
SEED (distribution)	442
HIV/AIDS (distribution)	488
Andean Counter-drug	727
Department of the Treasury	
Contributions to international financial institutions (IFIs)	1,383
Technical assistance and advice	19
Debt relief	94
Department of Agriculture	
PL-480 II (budget)	1,185
U.S. Agency for International Development	
DA, child survival, disaster	4,511
Millennium Challenge Corporation	994
Peace Corps	308
InterAmerican Foundation	16
African Development Foundation	19
White House	
Emergency Fund for Complex Crises	100
Iraq reconstruction[a]	18,439
Other departments and agencies[b]	500–1,000

a. Iraq reconstruction funding is considered a one-time exceptional financing program.
b. This is an estimate since data are not available for the technical assistance and other programs funded abroad by non-foreign affairs agencies. In 1994 OMB estimated about this amount for these expenditures. Thus the amount reflected here could be construed as conservative.

USAID has been the principal foreign assistance agency of the federal government for the past forty-five years. It is responsible, in consultation with the Department of State, for the policies, country allocations, and uses of development assistance (used to promote economic growth, education and agricultural development, health and family planning and democracy, conflict prevention and humanitarian assistance), "child survival" (programs aimed at improving the health and well-being of children), and disaster relief and recovery. USAID is usually consulted on policies and allocations of aid monies under the Economic Support Fund (ESF), Support for Eastern Europe Democracy Act (SEED), Newly Independent States (NIS), Andean counter-drug programs, and a portion of the president's major new HIV/AIDS initiative, or President's Emergency Plan for AIDS Relief (PEPFAR), and also is involved in implementing a significant portion of these programs.

Aid programs in the Department of State include funding for refugee programs abroad, U.S. voluntary contributions to international organizations and programs involved in some aspect of development work (for example, the United Nations Development Program), and the policy and allocative responsibilities for ESF (grant aid originally intended to ease the burden of security expenditures for U.S. friends and allies abroad—especially in the Middle East—but increasingly used to fund a number of other activities associated with relief and reconstruction, development, and democracy promotion). In 2004 a new Office of the Coordinator for Reconstruction and Stabilization, reporting to the secretary of state, was established to lead government planning and engagement in failed and failing states and in postconflict situations. There are at least seven State Department coordinators in assistance-related areas with a combined staff of approximately 215. These include coordinators to provide policy leadership to support economic and political transitions in former socialist countries in Eastern Europe and in the former Soviet Union; a coordinator for a new aid initiative in the Middle East—the Middle East Partnership Initiative (MEPI)—that aims to support economic, political, and educational reform efforts with a special focus on women and youth; and a coordinator (and funding) for PEPFAR. Further, the Department of State manages program funding for "alternative development," seeking to persuade coca farmers in the Andes to shift to producing other crops or find other means to earn their living; and directs the Human

Rights and Democracy Fund. The implementation of most of these programs rests with USAID and, at times (especially with HIV/AIDS), with other government agencies with expertise in needed areas.

The Department of the Treasury is responsible for managing U.S. participation in the World Bank, the International Monetary Fund, and the regional development banks. It is also responsible for government policies involving debt relief and maintains its own technical assistance program ($19 million in fiscal 2005) to advise other governments on taxes, fiscal policy, and issues associated with implementing significant economic reforms. In the past, USAID led the U.S. delegations to Consultative Group and other donor meetings, but these responsibilities have now shifted for the most part to the departments of State and Treasury.

The Department of Agriculture funds grants of food aid for humanitarian and development purposes, which are administered by USAID. These grants, first passed by Congress in 1954 as Public Law 480 (Title II), provide food (for example, wheat, rice, and cooking oil) in response to emergencies and disasters around the world through both the World Food Programme and private voluntary organizations. They amounted to $1.2 billion in 2004. One other small food aid program—the McGovern-Dole International Food for Education and Childhood Nutrition Program—was funded at $87 million in the same year. While the responsibility for Title II resides with USAID, budget decisions continue to be shared by USAID and the U.S. Department of Agriculture on the McGovern-Dole food aid program.

The Millennium Challenge Corporation (MCC), the newest agency in the U.S. government aid firmament, was established in 2003 to manage (eventually) $5 billion per year in aid funds. In fiscal year 2004, $994 million was appropriated, in fiscal year 2005, $1.5 billion, and for fiscal year 2006, the president has requested $3 billion. The MCC is intended to focus aid entirely on promoting economic growth and poverty alleviation, targeting governments of low- and middle-income countries with a demonstrated commitment to democracy, free markets, and investment in people. It is also expected to deliver the aid in new ways—for instance, by creating a contractual relationship between the MCC and the recipient government with clear and measurable goals and performance commitments for each party. The MCC signed its first agreement with a recipient government (Madagascar) in March 2005 for $110 million.

The Peace Corps places U.S. volunteers in developing and transition countries to provide advice, manage community-based projects, and teach a variety of subjects in schools. The Inter-American Foundation and the African Development Foundation both fund discrete, community-based activities in their respective regions.

The State Department proposed in 2005 a new aid program—a fund of $100 million to meet "complex foreign contingencies"—allowing the administration to respond to or prevent impending crises such as ethnic wars, interstate conflicts, mass killings, or genocide. These monies are not intended to be used for natural disasters (for which funds are available from USAID). The program was not funded in fiscal 2005, but the administration has requested $100 million in fiscal 2006 for the Conflict Response Fund to be administered by the secretary of state.

Other federal departments and agencies typically have their own international assistance programs—though they do not describe them as such. These programs provide technical assistance and advice to foreign governments and, at times, finance activities in their particular areas of responsibility. For example, the Department of Labor supports a number of projects abroad, often managed by NGOs, aimed at reducing child labor by expanding opportunities for formal and informal education, as well as a program on education and awareness of HIV/AIDS in the workplace in Burkina Faso, Cameroon, China, Indonesia, Sri Lanka, and Trinidad and Tobago. The Department of Health and Human Services, through its Atlanta-based Centers for Disease Control, provides advice, disease surveillance, and response services to poor countries. The Environmental Protection Agency offers technical assistance to other governments, again often through nongovernmental organizations, on conservation, pollution problems, and other environmental issues. In fact, USAID estimates that some fifty other federal government units carry out aid-related activities overseas today.[10] Some of these programs are sufficiently complex or large that their home agencies assign personnel abroad to oversee them. The report of the Overseas Presence Advisory Panel, published in 1999, noted that "thirty executive branch agencies now have important statutory responsibilities that require an overseas presence."[11] While data on U.S. government expenditures are rarely kept in accounts labeled "international assistance" or "foreign technical assistance," it appears from various studies and information on government departments' and agencies' websites that these expenditures have grown rapidly over the past decade or so and may total between $500 million and $1 billion.[12]

In the fragmented structure of U.S. international assistance today, no single entity systematically plans and assesses the effectiveness of these programs together. U.S. ambassadors often have a good sense of the extent of aid and other programs in the countries where they serve, but this is not guaranteed, as is clear in the Overseas Presence Advisory Panel report cited above. And in reality, these U.S. ambassadors sometimes have limited influence over what other U.S. government agencies do in the countries in which they serve. "Several Ambassadors told the Panel that they frequently receive multiple instructions for initiatives, all with high priority, but without any rank order established for them."[13] On the basis of these and other findings, the Overseas Presence Advisory Panel described U.S. overseas presence as "near a state of crisis. . . . Conflicting directions and lack of intergovernmental coordination in Washington hinder cooperation at overseas missions—even when addressing a common problem. . . . In other cases, there are conflicting priorities."[14]

The 2002 National Security Strategy and the 2004–09 USAID–State Department Strategic Plan are both attempts to rationalize the international programs of multiple agencies, but neither strategy addresses issues raised by the many other U.S. government entities working overseas. For example, the Department of Defense (with limited experience in postconflict community development and recovery) has been directing reconstruction activities in Afghanistan through Provincial Reconstruction Teams, while USAID (with considerable background in postconflict work) has been struggling to obtain adequate funding for essential community-based reconstruction and organization in that country.

Different agencies bring different policies and regulations to the task. A case in point: CDC implements programs overseas for both the Department of Health and Human Services, its "mother" agency (which has considerably expanded overseas funding in recent years), while also working with funds it receives from the State Department's HIV/AIDS coordinator and from USAID. The result: CDC must follow two or three very different sets of regulations governing the same program in the same country.

The high transaction costs associated with the current foreign aid structure also affect our allies, as officials from other aid-giving governments and international organizations try to figure out whom to contact within the U.S. government on issues of common concern. But the diffuse responsibility for implementing development assistance is only one element in the fragmentation in U.S. international assistance. Another involves the dispersion of responsibility for budgeting and policy among agencies. For example:

—Title II food aid is located in the budget of the Department of Agriculture, but decisions on the allocation and use of that aid, as noted above, are made primarily by USAID.

—Decisions on the country allocation and use of ESF monies are made primarily in the Department of State and implemented by USAID.

—Decisions on the distribution of funds among federal government agencies for Eastern Europe and the former Soviet Union, MEPI, and, most recently, HIV/AIDS programs are made by coordinators in the Department of State, while implementation is the responsibility of USAID and other government agencies receiving funding.

In some cases, aid agencies are jointly governed by several government agencies and departments. The Inter-American Foundation and the African Development Foundation are both governed by boards of directors that include several senior federal government officials, as well as private individuals. The new Millennium Challenge Corporation is governed by a board that includes the secretaries of the departments of State and of the Treasury, USAID, the Office of the U.S. Trade Representative, and four private individuals representing various stakeholder groups engaged in aid issues.

Figure 3 attempts to capture the complex relationships in the structure of U.S. international assistance. The agencies involved in budget and policy decisions on aid programs, and sometimes their implementation, are at the top. Along the bottom are the various aid programs themselves.

Other U.S. Agencies and Programs Related to Development

Providing foreign aid is not the only way the U.S. government attempts to influence development abroad. Debt relief, trade policies, and investment programs can also have a major impact on other countries' welfare. Responsibilities for these policies and programs rest with a variety of government agencies. The Office of the U.S. Trade Representative (USTR) takes the lead on international negotiations involving trade issues. Its development-related programs include the Generalized System of Preferences, African Growth and Opportunity Act, Andean Trade Partnership Act, and the Caribbean Basin Initiative. In addition to these programs, the expanding number of U.S. bilateral free trade area agreements and the World Trade Organization–sponsored trade negotiations called the Doha Round also have significant implications for developing countries. Free trade agreements (in addition to NAFTA) have been negotiated or are under serious consideration for Andean countries, Central American countries, Israel, Singapore, Jordan, Morocco, Chile, Panama, and the South African Customs Union; free trade proposals are also on the table for all of the Americas, the Middle East, Asian countries, and other regional groupings. The U.S. Trade Representative often relies on

FIGURE 3. *Selected Federal Agencies Responsible for Distributing Foreign Aid*

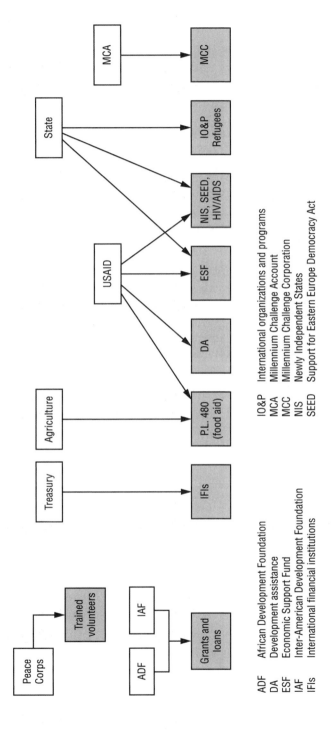

ADF African Development Foundation
DA   Development assistance
ESF Economic Support Fund
IAF Inter-American Development Foundation
IFIs International financial institutions

IO&P International organizations and programs
MCA Millennium Challenge Account
MCC Millennium Challenge Corporation
NIS Newly Independent States
SEED Support for Eastern Europe Democracy Act

USAID to provide technical assistance to help a country carry out the agreements it has negotiated with the United States but does not provide resources to enable USAID to do so.

The Trade and Development Agency offers grants for feasibility studies, technical assistance, training, and orientation activities intended to promote an expansion of trade with developing countries. The Overseas Private Investment Corporation operates a number of programs encouraging U.S. firms to invest in developing countries. The Export-Import Bank encourages and finances the sale of U.S. manufactures abroad, including to developing countries. The Department of Agriculture does the same for food and fiber products. The Treasury Department oversees debt restructuring programs for heavily indebted poor countries. In short, a wide range of government agencies manage programs that have profound impacts on the economies of developing countries—as, for example, is the case with domestic agricultural price supports that harm the exports of otherwise competitive food and fiber producers in poor countries. Sometimes these programs are coordinated with the agencies concerned with foreign policy, for example, when USAID provides technical assistance to countries engaged in free trade negotiations with the USTR. Often they are not.

Implications of Fragmentation

What are the strengths, weaknesses, and implications of the organizational landscape of U.S. international assistance today? One advantage of having a variety of aid agencies and programs is that they can bring diversity to the way the U.S. government uses its aid and how it is delivered abroad, enabling the government as a whole to apply its vast resources and expertise to a variety of issues in a large number of foreign countries. One bureaucracy may be more appropriate to certain foreign operations than another. Another advantage of this foreign aid packaging is that it helps ensure the more efficient flow of information on issues of relevance to different sectors of the United

States' economy (for example, disease outbreaks, droughts, or other natural disasters) than if all aid were filtered through a single agency. A third advantage is that it expands "ownership" within the federal government for maintaining a safe and prosperous place for the United States in the world. And a fourth is that, at least in theory, domestic agencies can bring new constituencies to the table in support of U.S. international engagement and assistance abroad.

However, given the extent of fragmentation in the nation's international assistance, weaknesses would appear to outweigh strengths. Such weaknesses include:

—danger of overlap and sometimes conflict among aid-funded activities, lessening the potential effectiveness of the aid;

—higher administrative and transaction costs associated with multiple aid organizations within the government (including U.S. embassies abroad);

—higher transaction costs for foreign governments (both aid recipients and other aid donors), U.S. partners in aid giving, and others associated with U.S. international assistance when looking for information, contacts, or appropriate agencies with which to coordinate their activities; and

—difficulties of managing aid for maximum impact within an overall policy and strategic framework and of evaluating and learning from the various experiences of aid interventions among different agencies.

There is also another potentially significant disadvantage associated with this fragmentation. Separating policy from implementation can reduce the mutual learning and exchange that comes when an agency is responsible for both—what will work in the political and substantive context of policymaking is one thing; what will work in actually implementing aid activities is often quite another. Where individuals responsible for these separate functions are required to collaborate—indeed, where they are responsible for and experienced in both policy and implementation—the professionalism and realism of aid policies and programs are likely to be greater and the effectiveness of the aid higher. Keeping policy and implementation functions together also encourages greater accountability and, thus, better care in the management of these functions generally. When they are separated, there is the danger that no one is responsible or accountable.

A variant of this last problem has plagued U.S. international assistance since it was established. Where aid has been *allocated* to countries (usually by the Department of State) primarily for diplomatic reasons—to fortify or reward a friendly state—but *implemented* (usually by USAID) to achieve developmental goals (for example, to expand education or promote agriculture), there has been a tendency in the executive branch, in Congress, in the media, in academe, and among the public to judge the effectiveness of the aid *solely* on its developmental impact. For example, critics have repeatedly pointed to the developmental failures and wastefulness in international assistance to such countries as the former Zaire, Egypt, Pakistan, and elsewhere where the quality of governance would have argued against providing large amounts of aid or any aid at all. Rarely is aid assessed from the point of view of its effectiveness in achieving its foreign policy goals, though in the cases of these countries (as well as others), diplomatic concerns were the decisive factors in determining whether these countries were aided and by how much.

Diplomatic purposes are valuable and legitimate uses of U.S. international assistance. But the impact of aid allocated primarily for those purposes should be assessed in terms of achieving diplomatic goals, especially in poorly governed countries where development outcomes may be in doubt.[15] The problem of separating decisions on the allocation of aid by the Department of State and its implementation by USAID has often led critics of foreign aid to blame USAID for the development failures of this type of aid (to the detriment of the reputation and morale of USAID) and, more broadly, to reach the mistaken conclusion that aid for development is generally ineffective.

One more point should be made regarding the consequences of the organization and, in particular, the bureaucratic location of federal international assistance programs. The two main U.S. government development agencies today—USAID and the MCC—are subcabinet-level agencies. They are thus not usually represented at cabinet-level discussions or—unless invited—at discussions by "principals" of foreign policy issues generally. USAID has, in the past, been invited to such discussions where aid-related issues are considered, but sometimes the invitation comes only after active lobbying by USAID officials and sometimes after basic policy decisions have been made. As a result, development concerns are not predictably part of policy discussions and decisions, for example, on trade, monetary, or security-related issues. Brian Atwood, who served as administrator of USAID between 1993 and 1999, recalled that the agency, despite his best efforts, was not included in high-level administration discussions of the proposed African Growth and Opportunities Act until Congress insisted that the development implications of the legislation be considered. He commented:

> I suspect that there were many lost opportunities to influence policy by providing the development perspective at the policy table. These occurred both because AID had a small policy staff that was not integrated into the interagency process and because the larger departments did not know what they did not know about development. In addition, State had no interest in inviting AID to its own table when large interagency issues loomed.[16]

The Evolution of the Structure of U.S. International Assistance

What has given rise to the complicated structure of U.S. international assistance today? The answer is some planning and a lot of organizational improvisation. The foundation for the current organization of foreign aid was laid by President John Kennedy in 1961, when he reshaped the way the government managed its aid programs, combining two existing bilateral organizations (the Development Loan Fund and the International Cooperation Agency) into the new Agency for International Development. The rationale President Kennedy presented for the reform of international assistance is as relevant today as it was forty-four years ago:

> For no objective supporter of international assistance can be satisfied with the existing program—actually a multiplicity of programs. Bureaucratically fragmented, awkward and slow, its administration is diffused over a haphazard and irrational structure covering at least four departments and several other agencies. The program is based on a series of legislative measures and administrative procedures conceived at different times and for different purposes, many of them now obsolete, inconsistent, and unduly rigid and thus unsuited for our present needs and purposes. Its weaknesses have begun to undermine confidence in our effort both here and abroad.[17]

At the time of the creation of USAID, discussions ensued inside and outside government on the best location for the new organization—whether it should be separate from the Department of State and whether it should be a cabinet-level agency. It was finally decided to create a semi-autonomous, subcabinet-level agency with a close relationship to the Department of State to reflect the mix of purposes of U.S. aid at that time—to support a policy of cold war containment primarily through helping poor countries to develop economically. It was recognized that the mission of managing U.S. foreign relations—emphasizing government-to-government contacts and negotiations—was sufficiently different from the mission of promoting development—involving economic, social, and political change and often involving nongovernmental organizations—to justify the existence of separate agencies. But the two purposes needed to be associated bureaucratically because they were related substantively. For that reason, a separate, semi-independent, subcabinet-level aid agency was created as the best (or least bad) arrangement to manage U.S. bilateral aid. Responsibility for U.S. participation in international financial institutions such as the World Bank and the Inter-American Development

Bank was already lodged in the Treasury Department and left there by the Kennedy administration.

Over time, other aid agencies were created. The Peace Corps, which President Kennedy had intended to be part of USAID, was established by Congress as a separate agency. In the early 1970s, the Inter-American Foundation was created, and, in the early 1980s, an African Development Foundation was established. At times, new programs and agencies were created to serve purposes not already addressed by existing agencies or to raise the priority and prominence of existing functions. At other times, aid programs were set up for primarily domestic political objectives—to meet the demands of influential members of Congress or prominent groups. On occasion, they just emerged to meet urgent tasks.

Over the past decade, the federal government has continued to expand the number of aid agencies and programs. Non-foreign affairs agencies of the U.S. government have gotten involved in giving assistance; as noted, a new organization—the MCC—has been created; the Department of State has greatly expanded its policy and operational engagement in aid giving, as have Treasury, the USTR, and nearly all other major federal departments. What is behind this trend? In part, it reflects the phenomenon of globalization, including the globalization of federal agencies whose interests and responsibilities can no longer be entirely contained within the country's borders. In part, it reflects the evolving purposes of international assistance: newly prominent goals such as furthering economic and social transitions in former socialist bloc countries, addressing global problems such as the spread of infectious diseases, grappling with, preventing, and mediating conflict and postconflict recovery, and promoting democracy abroad have energized government agencies that previously were disengaged from the international assistance arena. Finally, the trend toward multiplying U.S. government aid programs and agencies reflects an organizational response to apparent dissatisfaction with USAID, which has been seen by many inside and outside the government over the past decade or so as slow, unresponsive, and difficult to reform.

Reorganizing U.S. International Assistance

There have been several major efforts to reorganize the overall structure of international assistance since the Kennedy administration. There have been many more efforts to reform USAID itself—indeed, the history of the agency is in part a tale of attempts to improve performance and lessen criticisms of international assistance by changing the programmatic focus, altering operational systems, and reorganizing units involved in policy and delivery of assistance. A quick review of the history of initiatives to reform the overall structure of U.S. foreign assistance, the dissatisfactions that gave rise to the reform, and the reasons for their success or lack thereof are necessary background for any discussion of reform today.

The creation of USAID in 1961 was itself the first major effort at organizational reform (though a variety of less sweeping efforts had preceded it). Dissatisfaction with USAID's predecessor agencies, the International Cooperation Administration and the Development Loan Fund, centered on both the lack of focus on poverty reduction as a primary goal and the politicization of the choice of aid recipients. The Foreign Assistance Act of 1961, which established the Agency for International Development, restructured assistance around two broad program mechanisms: the Development Loan Fund, geared to investments in capital infrastructure, and the Development Grant Fund, focused on poverty reduction and human resource development in the poorest countries. It created a guaranty program that later became the Overseas Private Investment Corporation (OPIC), to provide political risk insurance for American companies doing business overseas, and the Supporting Assistance Program that later became the Economic Support Fund, to promote economic and political stability in countries where U.S. security interests were compelling.

The first attempt to reorganize USAID occurred during the Nixon administration. The president, reacting to rising criticisms from Congress and findings of various studies at the time, recommended that

USAID be eliminated and three new bilateral aid agencies be created—one to manage aid loans, one to fund development-related research and technical assistance, and one to coordinate aid, trade, and related policies affecting developing countries. This complicated and ambitious proposal went nowhere in Congress and the administration did not press it.

By the beginning of the 1970s, public dissatisfaction with foreign assistance found expression in other types of congressional inquiry and criticism. Concern focused on both how effective development investments were and how resources were used for short-term political purposes, such as indirectly supporting the increasingly unpopular war effort in Indochina, rather than the longer term effort at poverty reduction—an overriding goal in the view of many in the development community.

The Foreign Assistance Act was amended in 1973 to address these concerns and provided for direct assistance to address basic human needs among the "poorest of the poor" in the developing world. Instead of reforming funding mechanisms (for example, loans and grants), the legislation focused USAID on the question of "who benefits" and on broad program categories (education, agriculture, health, and family planning). Technical assistance replaced budget support and infrastructure funding as the focus for USAID programs, and USAID created functional bureaus to supplement the geographic bureaus.

By the end of the 1970s, concern over increasing aid fragmentation led Senator Hubert Humphrey to introduce a bill creating an International Development Cooperation Agency (IDCA). This was the first attempt to bring together development functions, both those housed outside USAID—for example, OPIC and entities contributing to United Nations agencies and the multilateral banks—and those such as food aid and development assistance for which USAID was wholly or in part responsible. The director of IDCA was to be a subcabinet-level office whose authorities came directly from the president—not through the secretary of state as before. Even though Humphrey's bill never passed the Senate, the Carter administration attempted to enact some of its ideas. It did create an "IDCA" but with only coordinating responsibilities over existing aid programs and nominal authorities over programmatic, budgetary, and personnel decisions. IDCA had limited impact and was formally abolished in 1999.

In the late 1980s another attempt to rewrite U.S. foreign assistance was launched by the House Committee on Foreign Affairs. Seeking to address the proliferation of program priorities and the apparent lack of evidence of program impact, the Hamilton-Gilman bill (Representatives Lee Hamilton and Benjamin Gilman) attempted to streamline congressional oversight as well as focus USAID on four broad themes: economic growth, poverty alleviation, environmental sustainability, and promotion of political pluralism. This effort did not result in enacted legislation, nor did subsequent attempts to rewrite the authorizing legislation within the executive branch throughout the early 1990s. But it did reflect continuing concern within government circles about the need to streamline processes, limit the scope of programs, focus on results, and address the poor understanding of the nature, size, and purpose of international assistance among the American people.

Three other efforts at restructuring U.S. foreign assistance bear mentioning. Reflecting the centrality of such assistance to U.S. foreign policy, in 1994 and 1995 the Department of State proposed to consolidate several foreign affairs agencies within the department— USAID, the U.S. Information Agency, and the Arms Control and Disarmament Agency. The latter two agencies were eventually merged into the State Department, but after fierce resistance on the part of USAID, Vice President Gore, who was spearheading an effort to streamline and make federal agencies more accountable at the time, agreed to the agency's independence but recommended closer reporting links between its administrator and the secretary of state. The proposal for "merger" of USAID into State was then taken up in the Senate by the chair of the Senate Foreign Relations Committee, Jesse Helms, but President Clinton resisted the idea and it went nowhere. The arguments for including USAID in the State Department were based on two beliefs: that, as a tool of U.S. foreign policy, foreign assistance needed to be more closely and directly managed by the secretary of state and that the merger would raise the profile of foreign assistance through a cabinet-level secretary. The arguments against the incorporation focused on the significant differences in missions, functions, staffing, and management operations between a development agency and one focused on diplomacy.

The second attempt at restructuring involved the redrafting of the Foreign Assistance Act in 1993–94 during the Clinton administration. One of the most striking aspects of the Peace, Prosperity, and Democracy Act, which was never passed, was an attempt to recast funding for international assistance strictly along program lines and to bundle related programs of a number of agencies (for example, by pulling together all funding for international health, now spread across USAID and many other departments including State, Health and Human Services, and Labor).

The latest attempt at a major reorganization of federal foreign assistance came in 2002 with the announcement of the creation of the MCC, an independent agency mentioned earlier with a separate budget and personnel, and with funding focused on a limited number of countries seen to "rule justly, invest in their people, and encourage economic freedom." A separate agency was justified, proponents explained, because the goals and the way the new funds were to be managed were different from the way USAID operated. As of today, the challenges of setting up and running a new agency, establishing its working relationships with others (especially USAID and State), responding to members of Congress, as well as groups and interests outside government with a stake in its operation—not to mention foreign governments—*and* demonstrating results in a relatively limited amount of time are significant.

Structure and Processes of the U.S. Agency for International Development

Any organization that directs programs "in the field"—that is, distant from headquarters—and finances activities in different technical areas, must find a balance between the authorities of headquarters and the field as well as between management and programs or, more precisely, between management personnel (to oversee activities and manage agency activities generally) and technical experts to ensure the appropriateness and quality of what is being delivered and to learn and innovate.

From its creation as the principal international assistance arm of the federal government, USAID has had a field-oriented structure, with a sizeable portion of its direct-hire personnel—both technical and managerial—assigned overseas, assisted by personal services and other contractors and foreign nationals, with considerable (though far from complete) authority to plan and oversee aid interventions.[18] By contrast, the MCC reflects a different management approach and is almost exclusively headquarters driven. The purpose of USAID field missions is both to shape programs designed by the agency to address local needs and opportunities, thereby diminishing the risk of failure or ineffective aid, and to oversee implementation. Because of its field presence, USAID can bring an understanding of field realities (and what will work) that other agencies do not have, and for this reason USAID may be called upon to implement programs of the State Department, the MCC, or other U.S. government entities.

USAID's field structure remains intact today, although the size and functions of the field missions have shifted. Today, missions—which now number seventy-five—are considerably smaller, with no more than seven or eight professionals (and often fewer) on staff, many of whom are management and support staff, such as controllers, lawyers, executives, and budget officers. This staff downsizing and consequent shift in the work assigned to overseas personnel reflect the agency's realities. It has become more of a manager or "wholesaler" of aid programs (that is, outsourcing the planning and implementation of aid-funded activities), rather than a "retailer" (that is, designing and implementing its own programs and projects). Indeed, in many cases, USAID has become a wholesaler to wholesalers—letting large contracts for aid work, usually to consulting firms, which then subcontract much of the work to other firms or NGOs. These shifts in the way the agency does business have caused it to reexamine its mission structure, functions, and professional personnel requirements. For example, if USAID is called on less to design and deliver development programs or advise governments on policies, is a significant field presence still warranted? Or perhaps is a different field structure appropriate?[19] If the function of USAID missions is to understand and engage with the local society and polity, should there be more technical personnel in the field with the time, responsibility, language, and other skills to undertake such activities? These questions, raised both within and outside USAID, also relate to how the federal government wishes to try to shape events and conditions in the countries it helps.

As noted above, because the proportion of technical personnel in USAID has declined, the agency has increasingly relied on external sources for its technical advice, as have other parts of the government. Several factors have contributed to this shift:

—career incentives within the government that favor those who manage large budgets and staffs rather than those who provide technical advice,

—programmatic preference (reinforced by Congress) for service delivery rather than research and policy analysis (the latter generally requiring greater specialized expertise), and

—general downsizing of government leading to reductions in the number of direct-hire government employees.

The smaller USAID has become in terms of direct-hire staffing, the higher the premium it has placed on management staff over the more specialized and less interchangeable technical staff. This trend toward outsourcing technical expertise raises questions about the extent to which USAID, or any public agency, can remain a leader and innovator—a "knowledge agency"—if it no longer has the in-house technical capacity to learn and innovate. Questions such as these have led the administration to launch an initiative aimed at strengthening USAID's workforce and rebuilding its management and technical capacity. These changes affecting USAID—driven less by careful planning than by ad hoc accommodations to resource scarcities, caps on personnel levels, and other constraints—suggest that the time is right for USAID to examine how it is organized and staffed to achieve its mission abroad more effectively, especially in view of the diversity of the development challenges and opportunities in the twenty-first century.

Programming Processes

Any agency responsible for programming public resources needs to adopt processes to ensure that decisionmaking is transparent and that the agency is accountable. USAID has instituted systems to accomplish these tasks, including strategic planning, results management, procurement, evaluation, and extensive reporting to Congress and the public. Many of these processes, however, are a poor fit with the real tasks of USAID today. This is not a new observation: it was made several decades ago by Judith Tendler in her insightful book *Inside Foreign Aid* and has only become more relevant since.[20] The basic reason has to do with the complex task environment involved in bringing about economic, social, and political changes in foreign countries.

Major challenges include

—the limited familiarity of aid officials and other policymakers (for example, the White House, Congress) with conditions (for example, cultural mores and attitudes, institutional relationships) in recipient countries,

—the experimental approaches and technologies required in developing country settings, and

—the essential (but not always enthusiastic or sustained) support and buy-in of the beneficiaries themselves required for program success and sustainability.

An uncertain task environment necessarily requires informed, innovative, flexible, and risk-taking behavior on the part of development assistance personnel and an open-minded and, to a considerable extent, an open-ended view of what constitutes positive (and negative) results.

As a result of the 1993 Government Performance and Results Act, all government agencies are required to program their funds through an elaborate strategic planning process with measurable indicators of results that are assessed annually. This process is demanding and rigorous but presents several fundamental problems for USAID. First, it is far too rigid: it is slow and cumbersome in operation; it can discourage innovation and risk taking; it can limit in time and scope the potentially beneficial outcomes of aid interventions; and it usually does not include "learning" as a specific and measurable result of aid interventions. Further, where indicators are used to track predetermined outcomes, learning can actually be discouraged when valuable achievements—or failures—outside of expected results are not even examined. There is also evidence that results-based strategic planning has discouraged more in-depth project and program evaluations by USAID.[21] Finally, USAID has at times compounded these problems by setting strategic objectives that are difficult to attain (or beyond its reach) in a limited time frame, leading to criticism from USAID's inspector general and the Office of Management and Budget.

USAID's current strategic planning process is also too control oriented and Washington driven, which the agency itself has recently recognized. It is virtually impossible for beneficiaries and the myriad stakeholders of U.S. assistance efforts to engage in the planning process in any meaningful way. The importance of beneficiary involvement is based on two insights: the first is that people will take more responsibility for things that they have been involved in creating—which they feel they "own"—than for activities decided and executed by outsiders. The second is that over the past half-century of aid giving, the governments and private organizations in many recipient countries have advanced significantly in their capacity to plan and execute development activities on their own. These advances are not uniform, of course. There are still truly "underdeveloped countries" and countries that are so miserably governed, so corrupt, or so troubled with conflict and insecurity that anyone who can flee does so—especially those with education. But this is no longer the norm, and USAID has had to develop new strategic planning guidance in an attempt to adapt its planning processes to this changing world.

In short, strategic planning processes designed for outcome-specific interventions with known technologies in well understood and stable environments, producing easily and quickly measurable results, may be appropriate for the Social Security Administration, but not for what are largely experimental activities intended to bring about societal changes in foreign countries with dynamic environments and, increasingly, effective organizations and educated people. Freeing U.S. assistance programs from the straightjacket of inappropriate regulations and unrealistic expectations and applying more relevant and meaningful systems are important management challenges for the administration and Congress.

Before considering options for reorganizing U.S. international assistance in the twenty-first century, it is important to look, first, at the unique domestic political context of U.S. international assistance. No other aid-giving government operates in such a complex and challenging political environment. Understanding this environment is important for understanding the past and shaping U.S. aid for the future. It also is useful to consider how other major donor governments have organized their aid-giving operations. And finally, it is worth spending some time exploring the probable world of the twenty-first century as it affects international assistance.

The Political Context of U.S. International Assistance

Institutions matter, including the political institutions through which key decisions are made about international assistance. Of all major aid-giving countries, the U.S. government has the only fully presidential system, with clearly separate legislative, executive, and judiciary branches. Most other donor governments are parliamentary democracies in which the executive is drawn from one or more parties in the legislature. The separation of Congress from the executive in the United States plus the authority vested in Congress to initiate, approve, amend, or veto legislation—including the all-important legislation appropriating funding for government spending programs—and congressional responsibility for oversight of such programs, give the Senate and the House of Representatives considerable influence over all aspects of U.S. international assistance. Indeed, Congress plays a far greater role in influencing federal aid than any legislature in any other aid-giving country. It influences overall policy directions, such as the priority given to supporting microenterprise or the shape and extent of family planning activities funded with U.S. aid. It influences which countries receive aid and how much they receive. It often decides how much aid is used for particular purposes and sometimes even determines the amount of aid provided to particular organizations implementing aid programs.

Congress makes its influence felt through legislative earmarks (that require the expenditure of aid monies for particular purposes); "directives" (congressional preferences for the expenditure of aid funds, usually recorded in oversight committee reports and often as politically exigent as earmarks); oversight hearings, required reporting, notifications (through which a government agency advises Congress that it wishes to use aid in ways not originally included in its proposals to Congress); and informal contacts among members of Congress, their often powerful staffs, and executive branch aid officials (see accompanying box).

There are, in addition, administration policy directives (often in the form of presidential initiatives), which similarly limit programmatic flexibility in the field. In recent years these have included presidential initiatives for

—Ending Hunger in Africa

—Central America Free Trade Agreement

—Digital Freedom Initiative

—TRADE in Africa

—Africa Education Initiative

—Centers for Excellence in Teacher Training

—Congo Basin Forestry Initiative

—Global Climate Change

—Water for the Poor

—Clean Energy Initiative

Earmarks and directives are not particular to foreign aid. They are commonly a part of U.S. government spending programs, a means of ensuring that congressional views are taken seriously, a vehicle for directing resources to groups and organizations favored by key members of Congress and their staffs, and a basis for putting together a coalition of votes sufficient to pass annual appropriations bills. For a program such as international assistance—never especially popular in Congress or among the public and often of relatively low political priority for presidents (many of whom have proven reluctant even to mention it in important speeches or to lobby for it with members of Congress)—earmarks and directives have played an important role in coalition building.

What influences the earmarks and directives imposed by Congress? The particular views and interests of individual members and their staffs play a role. The preferences of their constituents also often play a role, especially where constituent groups are well organized, are politically sophisticated, and can write, call, and contact members directly as well as contribute to their re-election campaigns. Additionally,

Development Assistance: Congressional Earmarks and Directives, 2005

Millions of dollars (amounts in parentheses are included in the total for program)

	Total
Child Survival—$1.6 billion	
Child Survival/Maternal Health	345
Polio (32)	
Vulnerable Children	30
HIV/AIDS	350
AIDS vaccine (27)	
Microbicides (30)	
International Partnership for Microbicides (2)	
Other infectious diseases	200
Malaria (90)	
TB (80)	
Family Planning	375
Global Fund	250
Development Assistance—$1.4 billion	
Agriculture, Economic Growth, Education, Environment	300
International Fertilizer Development Institute (4)	
World Food Program (6)	
International Real Property Foundation (1)	
Basic Education (300)	
American Schools and Hospitals (20)	
U.S. Telecommunications Training Institute (1)	
Environment	
Congo Basin Forestry Initiative (18)	
Office of Energy and Info Technology (15)	
Victims of Torture	10
Microenterprise	200
Trade Capacity Building	194
Women's Leadership Capacity	15
Laos	2
Haiti	25
Afghanistan	980
Reforestation (2)	
Human Rights (2)	
Women and Girls (50)	
Women-led NGOs (8)	
El Salvador	27
Guatemala	11
Honduras	22
Nicaragua	27
Liberia	6
Sudan	311
Clean Energy Initiative	180
Plant Biotechnology (25)	
Drinking Water (200)	
Water Missions International (2)	

Source: U.S. House of Representatives, *Making Appropriations for Foreign Operations, Export Financing and Related Programs for the Fiscal Year Ending September 2005 and for Other Purposes*, Conference Report to accompany H.R. 4818, November 2004, pp. 985–1032. Child Survival Programs and Development Assistance are two of several major U.S. bilateral aid programs. ESF and aid for Eastern Europe and the former NIS are also heavily earmarked. Some of the above earmarks and directives reflect administration proposals; many originate with members of Congress.

Washington lobbyists play a role in congressional actions on international assistance, representing foreign governments, U.S. corporate enterprises, business organizations, and others. Public interest and ethnic, religious, and national affinity groups lobby for aid for their particular interests (for example, environmental conservation) or a favored country, often with considerable impact. Perhaps the strongest among all these groups and organizations in terms of effectiveness has long been the American-Israel Public Affairs Committee (AIPAC), which has supported aid to Israel as well as international assistance generally. Many believe that without AIPAC, aid appropriations legislation over the past three decades could well have had a much more difficult time passing in an indifferent or hostile Congress.

Public opinion also plays a role in U.S. aid giving. But that role tends to be passive except when the public becomes aware of a major humanitarian crisis (for example, the 2004 Asian tsunami), at which time great public pressures can arise for a generous response by the U.S. government. According to public opinion polls in the United States and other aid-giving countries, a majority of Americans have long been supportive of aid in general (at around 55 percent over a number of years) but less so than publics in many other aid-giving countries, where support levels often range from 60 to 80 percent.[22] The U.S. public is also poorly informed about the size of federal aid, believing it is far more than it actually is.

What explains the traditionally low level of active public support within the United States for international assistance? The most obvious answer is the lack of information available to the U.S. public about development needs abroad, about the consequences for the United States of poverty abroad, or about the role of U.S. aid in addressing these issues. And one reason for this lack of information is undoubtedly the miniscule amount of public funds dedicated to educating the public about international or development issues—often called "development education." Most aid-giving governments spend some portion of their funding on informing their publics about development needs in poor countries and what their aid is doing abroad. In some cases, the development education programs fund conferences, curriculum materials for primary and secondary schools, national days focused on development, pairing up cities, provinces, private enterprises, and other organizations in developed countries with those in developing countries for mutual education and joint development efforts, and international visits and volunteer work by citizens of the aid-giving country in a developing country. The U.S. government has done relatively little of these sorts of activities in the past for a population that is the largest of any major aid-giving country in the world; and much of what it has done has been ad hoc. Development education, if it is to inform a public, needs to be continuous year after year.[23]

But there is another reason why the U.S. public has been less supportive of aid than the publics of many other aid-giving countries, such as Denmark, Germany, or the United Kingdom. These latter countries all have something of a "social democratic" tradition, with strong center-left parties and widely shared ideas that the rich should help the poor in their societies and that the state is an appropriate vehicle for that support. The United States has a much more limited social democratic orientation (evident to some extent in the New Deal) and a much greater tradition of classical liberal ideas that regard the state as a protector of liberties and property rather than a mechanism for wealth redistribution. For the Europeans, it was a short step from public aid and redistributive programs to benefit the poor at home to establishing such programs for poor countries abroad.

That step has been a much more contested one in the United States—for example, in the debate in the U.S. Senate on the occasion of the Irish potato famine in 1847. At that time, Senator Crittenden of Kentucky argued,

> The very abundance with which we are blessed increases our obligation to act generously, as well as charitably and justly, and to render obedience to the great law of humanity. . . . Tell me not of mere private and individual charity, when a whole nation

[that is, Ireland] is asking for assistance. In such a case, let a nation answer the imploration. . . . There are no other means by which all can alike contribute for the relief of a nation's suffering and privations.[24]

Senator Fairfield of Maine responded that Crittenden

could not permit his generous impulses to blind his judgment and lead him to disregard his solemn obligations to support the Constitution. . . . The money in the treasury was not ours—it belonged to the people, whose servants and agents we were. We had no more right to appropriate it to purposes as private individuals [than] to lay our hands upon the property of our neighbors. . . . It was sufficient for this Government to attend to the relief of those who were constitutionally placed under its jurisdiction.[25]

The classical liberals won this argument, with the vocal support of President Polk who threatened to veto any public aid to the Irish on constitutional and libertarian grounds. By the end of the nineteenth century, public aid for relief had become a more widely accepted use of public resources. But when aid was proposed to stabilize and help develop the economies of other countries after World War II, many of the same objections were voiced, especially from the conservative side of American politics.

By the beginning of the twenty-first century, these views appear to be changing as private individuals and groups, including evangelical organizations (often on the right of the political spectrum), become more involved in aid giving. What is not changing, however, is the limited tolerance for aid that is seen as wasted, used for corrupt purposes, or just plain ineffective. President Bush was able to justify and obtain a large increase in U.S. foreign aid for the Millennium Challenge Account because he assured Americans that monies would be more effective at reducing poverty by going only to governments already fulfilling a number of the conditions regarded as essential for aid effectiveness (that is, supporting free markets, good governance, and low levels of corruption). Has this promise been kept? At this stage, the program is still too new to say for sure.

Alternative Approaches: Other Aid-Giving Donor Countries

Because aid programs of other donor countries developed in a manner similar to those of the United States—a mix of planning, history, and improvisation—no single major aid-giving government has organized itself exactly like any other. There are, however, some broad organizational models.

One model is a cabinet-level, fully unified aid agency, encompassing all major aid programs, combining policy and implementation responsibilities, and including expertise in other areas of policy affecting development (for example, trade and investment). The one example of this model is the United Kingdom and its Department for International Development (DFID), a cabinet-level agency charged with furthering development abroad and responsible for both bilateral and multilateral aid programs. By most accounts, DFID is among the more effective and efficient aid agencies and appears to wield considerable influence within the British government over issues associated with development.[26]

Another chief example of a cabinet-level aid organization is Germany. In 1961, as a result of coalition politics, the German government established a Ministry of Development. The BMZ (Bundesministerium für Wirtschaftliche Zusammenarbeit und Entwicklung) bears responsibilities for German development policies but not their implementation. This is divided between the Kreditanstalt für Wiederaufbau (KfW), which manages capital investments and program loans, and the Deutsche Gesellschaft für Technische Zusammenarbeit (GTZ), which handles grants and technical assistance.

At the other extreme in terms of bureaucratic location are the aid programs of the Netherlands and Denmark, where the responsibilities for international assistance are fully integrated into the ministries of foreign affairs, including personnel, budgets, and representation in the field. A third model is represented by Japan and France, where aid is highly fragmented, with key policy and allocative decisions made by ministries of foreign affairs and of finance, and is implemented primarily by subcabinet-level aid agencies. Numerous other ministries in both countries also have their own aid programs. In France, where fragmentation grew out of colonial arrangements, there is no single government document today that describes all of the country's aid programs, although the government is reportedly working to create one.

Canada offers another model—one that has occasionally been proposed for U.S. aid. It has two subcabinet-level aid agencies, one responsible for research and technical assistance and the other for project and program loans and grants. This arrangement provides special protection and status for funding of development-related research.[27]

Most major aid agencies in any of these countries have adopted programming processes similar to those of USAID, including a variety of "results-based management" approaches, although they enjoy greater flexibility in allocating and managing their aid.[28] These include many of the following elements:

—white papers or major policy documents setting out the approaches and priorities of the agency in providing aid for development,

—studies of the overall development needs of recipient countries and of major sectors or global issues,

—strategic planning documents for recipient countries laying out the areas of intended intervention by the aid agency,

—project and program plans,

—contract- and grant-giving procedures, and

—monitoring, evaluation, and feedback processes.

In recent years, however, a number of donors have adopted a dramatically different approach to aid management. In an effort to streamline the diverse administrative requirements and to encourage recipient governments to take more responsibility for aid-funded activities, donor agencies have begun to pool their resources in Sector Wide Assistance Programs (SWAPs). Under a SWAP, an agency of the recipient government may produce an investment plan and submit it to a group of aid donors for approval; if the plan is approved, the donors support the proposal through their pooled funds and monitor its implementation. The United Kingdom, the Netherlands, Denmark, and others have begun to use the SWAP model where recipient governments have the capacity and probity to manage funds well. While the United States has not yet participated, it may adopt the SWAP approach with MCA monies.

Another tactic in aid giving is the "foundation" model. This approach involves the donor agency in establishing guidelines and indicating areas (for example, health or basic education) for projects or programs it is prepared to fund, and soliciting proposals from the recipient government, NGOs, private enterprises, or social entrepreneurs. While this method of funding is often used by the many private foundations funding development activities, as well as public foundations such as the Inter-American and African Development foundations in the United States and international organizations such as the Global Fund to Fight AIDS, Tuberculosis, and Malaria, it is rarely followed by government aid agencies, probably because it can carry high overhead costs (of reviewing, approving, and overseeing many small projects). [29] It also removes the donor agency from direct engagement in development policies and programming.

Foreign Aid in the Twenty-first Century

The context of aid giving in the twenty-first century will be very different from that of the last. The world of international assistance in coming years promises more diversity in the organizations involved in

+ cplxite et diversite do org   + diversi

development as well as in the sources of aid. It will have greater dynamism as the changes generated by technological advances and development achievements of the past play out and others emerge. Important new opportunities and several new challenges will influence the purposes and uses of international assistance. And it will play out in an arena where not only is there no clear leader or primus inter pares among development organizations but also where the United States must regain some level of trust and credibility as a serious development player.

Diversity and Density in Development: An Era of "Many to Many"

Over the past fifty years, international assistance has been almost entirely public aid—as defined here—from governments to governments, to international organizations, or, in relatively small amounts, to NGOs to be spent in poor countries. Some private transfers from large foundations (Ford, Rockefeller, Carnegie, and others) and private funds channeled through NGOs promoted economic and social progress in poor countries. But public aid was by far the largest source of concessional transfers from rich to poor countries. In the coming decades, the scenario will be different.

The sources of aid in this century will include a larger number of well-funded foundations, such as the Gates Foundation, George Soros's Open World Institute, or Ted Turner's UN Foundation. The Gates and Soros foundations alone spend around $1 billion annually on development-related activities abroad. Additionally, the number of foundations making grants internationally has increased—up 10 percent between 1998 and 2002 alone.[30]

What is less dramatic but growing in size is the role of venture philanthropists, individual and corporate aid givers, and the social entrepreneurs, small businesses, and NGOs in developing countries engaged in a myriad of development-related activities. Using the Internet, a number of U.S.-based NGOs—Netaid, the Acumen Fund, Giving Global, and others—have positioned themselves as intermediaries between individuals, groups, and enterprises that wish to make charitable contributions to development projects abroad, bypassing government and, at times, traditional NGOs. The tsunami disaster of 2004 alone gave an immense boost to Internet charitable giving and may have significantly expanded the number of people involved in private giving for international development. These new actors and opportunities will not only increasingly populate the landscape of financial assistance in coming years but will also influence the international agenda for giving, creating a world very different from the government-dominated practices so familiar in the twentieth century.

In addition to privately funded foundations, corporate enterprises themselves will play a larger and somewhat different role in development work abroad, on top of any direct foreign investment they may make. A number of large U.S. corporations (for example, GAP and Hewlett-Packard) have already begun to fund training and other development-related activities in poor countries, not only because such activities are good public relations—applauded by their clients, publics, employees, and boards of directors as signs of good corporate citizenship—but also because these programs help to develop their future workforce and customers and give corporations valuable insight into what goods and services to market eventually in these countries.[31]

International NGOs will continue to play an important role in international assistance, both implementing aid projects and programs and acting as advocates for aid and development within their own, largely rich countries. In fact, their advocacy role may well become more prominent as they increasingly act in coordinated, transnational networks in lobbying campaigns such as the Landmines Campaign or Jubilee 2000 (in support of debt cancellation). Such campaigns can and do influence the agenda for official development aid, as well as influence the purposes and direction of private aid giving.

Private individuals are likely to play an increased role in aid giving in the twenty-first century as well. Individuals with significant amounts of funding or name recognition (for example, musicians Bob

Geldof and Bono) and a desire to make a difference abroad have already claimed such a role, especially in times of humanitarian crises. Their role will continue and probably increase as an important source of influence on the size and direction of concessional resource transfers. With the continuing improvement in real-time information—even increasingly, real-time films and pictures—about human suffering in distant corners of the globe, other prominent individuals are sure to join them, as well as not-so-prominent ones who have resources and wish to do good in the world.[32]

Finally, there are remittances. These private transfers from immigrants in rich countries to their families in poor countries have grown to extraordinary levels in recent years. A new report by the Inter-American Development Bank estimated that in 2003 remittances from the United States to Latin America amounted to $30 billion.[33] That does not include remittances from immigrants in the United States to Africa, Asia, and the Middle East; nor does it include those from Europe or Japan to developing countries. But the growing movement of people from poor to rich countries has turned these transfers into major sources of capital for investment and consumption, with as much as 85 percent spent on consumer goods in recipient countries. When such goods result in better nutrition, health, and education for individuals, they contribute indirectly to development.[34] But increasingly, remittances have also contributed directly to community improvements. The federal, state, and local governments in parts of Mexico, for example, have created a program called Dos por Uno and Tres por Uno (Two for One or Three for One): for each remittance dollar used for infrastructure improvement, these various governments would match it with two or three additional dollars.[35] USAID has already begun to work with a number of organizations in Latin America to help channel remittances to development activities.

What these trends demonstrate is growth in both the diversity and density of groups and individuals engaged in development, private aid giving, and international resource transfers. We can expect to see more individuals, corporations, and community groups acting as independent development donors. Political stability in developed and developing countries, continuing prosperity in developed countries, rising incomes in less developed ones, and rapidly expanding access to information worldwide could easily contribute to an acceleration in development progress. As more groups become involved financially, the push for good governance, responsible economic management, and targeted assistance for the needy will grow.

The development challenges of the twenty-first century are likely to be as diverse as the array of development actors. Some formerly poor countries, such as South Korea, Costa Rica, and Tunisia, experienced rapid economic growth during the last half of the twentieth century and greatly reduced poverty, becoming "middle-income" countries. South Korea has now set up its own foreign aid program, amounting to nearly $300 million in 2002.[36] Others made considerable progress but with periodic setbacks, for example, Peru, Argentina, and Algeria. Some, including China and India, despite great but diminishing poverty, made remarkable economic progress. Yet others, such as Haiti and much of sub-Saharan Africa, seem to be stuck with almost intractable development problems. And finally, there are failed states such as Liberia, Sierra Leone, or Somalia, where governments cannot provide even minimal security for their populations. In countries where deprivation is widespread and economic progress minimal, where societies are poorly integrated and governance weak—and not a few countries in Africa, Central Asia, the Caucasus, and elsewhere fit this description—the outbreak of civil conflict and state failure remains a real possibility in the twenty-first century. The devastating impact of HIV/AIDS could become another cause of state failure, and there may be equally menacing diseases or environmental catastrophes awaiting us in the future.[37]

Each recipient country's particular circumstance will guide the nature of assistance, a notion recognized by the Bush administration in the creation of the MCC, as well as by USAID's efforts to develop a set of policies and instruments to address the problem of fragile and failed states. The needs of a country losing a fifth or more of its population to HIV/AIDS, for example, are significantly different from one whose governance, economic openness, and management make it eligible for MCC monies.

After taking into account the expected diversity and density of the actors, instruments, purposes, and recipients of U.S. financial aid in the twenty-first century, two facts remain: first, the United States needs to be able to function—and collaborate—effectively in a world of multiple development actors where U.S. aid programs may not be the most important or the best funded; and, second, the United States must be able to address diverse needs in recipient countries and serve a variety of purposes within the broader scope of U.S. foreign policy. In short, U.S. international assistance needs to be flexible, nimble, and innovative to function effectively in a world of diversity and change—in an emerging world of "many to many."[38]

Challenges and Opportunities: Recommendations and Options for Organizing U.S. Foreign Aid

This essay has identified promoting development abroad as an essential priority for U.S. foreign policy in the twenty-first century. It has described the principal instrument for realizing that goal—foreign aid—and has identified several prominent problems associated with U.S. foreign aid, including its fragmented organization, its cumbersome processes, and the limited efforts at educating the American public on development issues. The question now is what should be done to address these problems. We will deal with fragmentation and bureaucratic location separately.

Three solutions to the problem of fragmentation in U.S. aid and development policies are possible. One involves unifying all major aid programs in a single agency, including expertise on other policies and programs impacting development abroad—especially trade and investment policies and debt relief. The second option—less costly politically but also likely to be less effective overall—is simply to unify the two principal development aid agencies, USAID and the MCC. The third option is to make no changes in current aid-giving agencies but require robust and authoritative coordination and leadership from somewhere within the U.S. government.

Option 1: Unifying All Major Aid Programs

Organizational experts often argue that form should follow function. Applied to foreign aid, that precept implies that programs aimed at improving lives and livelihoods and promoting development in poor countries should be co-located in a single organization. This would include not only economic development aid but also aid for promoting democracy and strengthening weak states, supporting economic and political transitions, addressing global issues, and providing humanitarian relief and postconflict assistance, since all share a common orientation (supporting beneficial change abroad), a common approach to achieving their purposes (working with public and private organizations), and often overlapping requirements for technical expertise, including such skills as knowledge of diseases and how health systems work; knowledge of the role and importance of constitutions, legal systems, political parties, and the media; and experience with the causes of conflicts and how to provide relief and postconflict reconstruction (both physical and institutional).

Supporting and encouraging development abroad requires a variety of interventions—both top-down (for example, working with governments on health sector reforms) and grass roots (working with small communities to establish health clinics). Designing and implementing programs and mobilizing the expertise needed to oversee them are clearly easier if resources are combined in one agency rather than if they are scattered across independent agencies as they now are. A compelling argument can thus be made to bring together responsibilities for overseeing U.S. participation in the World Bank, the regional

FIGURE 4. *Unified Development Agency for the United States*

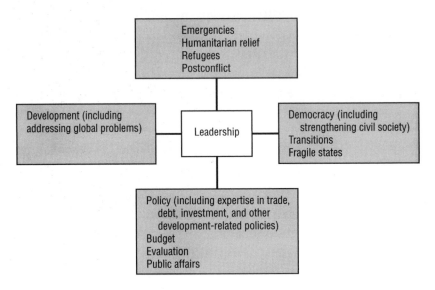

development banks, and UN development organizations (IFAD, UNICEF, UNIFEM, UNDP), with the expertise and programs of USAID, the MCC, the Inter-American and African Development foundations, and several relief and development-related programs now located in the Department of State.[39] One approach to organizing a unified aid agency might be based on categories of purposes, as shown in figure 4. The benefits of such an organizational approach would include both consistency in policy and message and efficiency in the use of scarce resources to promote international development.

This is but one organizational model. Others could be based on technical and regional bureaus or on bureaus set up according to the types of organizations from which they were drawn, for example, a bureau based on the MCC, on aid channeled through the international financial institutions, or on USAID's current portfolio.

Even with such a unified aid agency, the authority to make decisions on aid provided primarily for diplomatic purposes should rest with the Department of State or White House. The development agency could act, as USAID does today, as the implementing agency for aid programs *allocated* to countries for diplomatic reasons but *implemented* as development projects and programs. Accountability for the results of these programs, however, should rest both with the agency or department making the allocative decisions and with the agency implementing them to ensure that both the diplomatic and development purposes are understood and assessed separately. This would mean, for example, that when monies from the Economic Support Fund are provided for primarily diplomatic purposes, that aid should be evaluated both in terms of its diplomatic effectiveness and its developmental impact.

What about the proliferating aid programs in non-foreign affairs agencies? Ideally, where these programs duplicate the functions of the unified development agency, they should be transferred to the unified agency. At a minimum, they must be much more closely coordinated and not competitive with other federal government international development efforts.

A unified aid agency may be the best option for the long-run effectiveness of U.S. development policies and programs. But creating it would take time and involve significant political costs, as experience with the creation of a new Department of Homeland Security has demonstrated. Executive branch agencies losing programs—above all Treasury and State—would oppose such a move. Members of Congress would resist changes in programs to which they had a particular attachment. Constituencies outside of government might do the same. Further, such a change would require new authorizing legislation—at a minimum, where legislatively established agencies were merged into the unified aid agency. Achieving new, comprehensive authorizing legislation over foreign aid has, as noted earlier, been problematic at best. However, the ever-increasing prominence of development in U.S. foreign policy and the mounting resources being requested and appropriated for this purpose suggest that the benefits of a more coherent, efficient, and effective set of aid programs in a unified agency might be worth the political costs.

Option 2: More Modest Mergers

There are several less ambitious options that could reduce the clutter and improve the focus of U.S. international assistance efforts as well:

—Merge USAID and the MCC into a single economic development agency.

—Merge USAID into State to implement foreign policy–driven international assistance, and the Inter-American and African Development foundations into the MCC to implement "pure" economic development assistance.

—Leave all agencies intact, but strengthen the ability of the secretary of state to exercise his or her authorities under sections 1521–23 of the Foreign Affairs Reform and Restructuring Act of 1998 (included in Public Law 105-277) to coordinate all U.S. international assistance.

—Leave all agencies intact, but give the National Security Council the authority to coordinate assistance policy across the U.S. government.

Merge the MCC and USAID. A more modest approach to fragmentation would involve joining the two major aid agencies—the MCC and USAID. This at least would create a more coherent bureaucracy and encourage greater collaboration in program planning and implementation and better sharing of scarce technical resources. At the outset the MCC was created as a separate entity to ensure that it established a strategic vision and operating procedures distinct from those of USAID. It has begun to implement those procedures, with the naming of eligible and threshold countries and a variety of programming initiatives. It may be too early to put these two agencies under one roof, but if there were ways of protecting their separate modus operandi while avoiding the inevitable overlap and potential costs and conflicts associated with their separate existence, it would make good economic and management sense to proceed with a merger now, while USAID is rebuilding its technical and management expertise and the MCC is still developing its programs and processes.

Merge USAID with the State Department and the development foundations within the MCC. This option would hasten a policy drift that already appears under way—that is, the increasing number of aid programs directed and sometimes implemented by the Department of State. Folding USAID into State would bring the department more directly into the management of aid and further raise its prominence in this area. This approach would reduce duplication among programs such as humanitarian relief, addressing global problems, or democracy promotion that now exists both in USAID and State. It would strengthen the foreign policy orientation of these programs and potentially put more resources behind foreign policy priorities as well—an advantage in the eyes of many. But such a merger would carry costs. To work, it would eventually require the Department of State to establish in-house expertise in the technical fields relating to these programs and to acquire the program management skills associated with large-scale procurement and oversight responsibilities (both probably implying the creation of an additional "cone" in the foreign service or a civil service specialization).

Other potential costs could arise from the close identification that would inevitably occur between U.S. foreign policy and these State Department–funded aid programs in the field. With the widespread hostility in many parts of the world toward U.S. policies and the reluctance on the part of individuals and groups to be identified with those policies, this could be a significant problem. Aid from any U.S. government agency—or private U.S. agency for that matter—cannot entirely escape association with U.S. foreign policies, but an organization separate from the State Department and focused solely on improvement of economic and social conditions, such as USAID or MCC, may face less antagonism.

Finally, this option would separate assistance programs by purpose: those designed mainly to support U.S. foreign policy would be housed within the Department of State; those designed strictly to achieve development goals would be housed in the expanded MCC. Unfortunately, as noted in earlier sections, it is often very difficult to make such a clear-cut distinction, and the result would inevitably be similar to the current situation, with multiple U.S. aid programs coexisting in the same countries.

Strengthen the ability of the secretary of state to exercise her authorities to coordinate all U.S. international assistance. The principal attraction of this option is that it is likely to be the easiest to implement: the legislative authority already exists and because it does not require organizational changes among agencies, it is less likely to be resisted. This option would undoubtedly require a new secretariat within the Department of State, but even with new staff to implement this option, it will not be effective if it is not considered a very high priority by the secretary. Furthermore, the coordination authorities given the secretary of state in Public Law 105-277 do not include the multilateral development banks, or IFIs, overseen by the Treasury Department, the trade-related activities of the USTR, or the Commerce or Agriculture departments, or the aid activities of the non-foreign affairs agencies. The secretary would need to seek additional authorities to effect coordination among these agencies or accept that this is but a small step in the right direction.

Lodge responsibility for interagency coordination of U.S. international assistance in the National Security Council. With a strong presidential mandate (and it would not work without one), the NSC could be the best location within the executive branch to coordinate international assistance efforts across domestic and international affairs agencies. It may be the only locus able to ensure that U.S. defense, diplomacy, and development resources are truly optimized. However, better coordination alone, while always useful, is not likely to solve all of the problems of fragmentation. Without a sizeable staff and control over personnel and budgets, "coordinators" cannot wield much influence over the policies and programs of independent agencies.

None of the above options has dealt effectively with the proliferation of small aid programs in the non-foreign affairs agencies of the U.S. government. At a minimum, two additional initiatives must be undertaken. First, a new approach to accountability to determine the effectiveness of foreign assistance is needed—one that would separate aid extended for diplomatic purposes from that for development purposes. Second, the administration must begin to collect data on the totality of federal international aid expenditures (a task, perhaps, for Office of Management and Budget leadership), including those from non-foreign affairs agencies, and put into place effective interagency vehicles for ensuring at least limited coordination among these programs. Ensuring that this basic information on U.S. government international assistance expenditures is available to Congress is a first step toward bringing a better informed approach to U.S. foreign aid.

Location, Location, Location

If a more unified development aid agency (options 1 and 2 above) is required to achieve U.S. goals in the world, where should this more unified aid agency be located within the government? There are three possibilities:

—Create an independent, cabinet-level development agency.

—Create a separate subcabinet-level aid agency that is semidependent on the Department of State (for example, as USAID is now, but taking foreign policy guidance from the Department of State).

—Locate the aid agency within the Department of State.

Establish a Department of International Development. Over the past year, recommendations for establishing an independent department have come from several sources, including the Commission on Weak States and National Security, a bipartisan panel of thirty former government officials, senior business leaders, academics, and NGO representatives, in its report *On the Brink: Weak States and National Security*.[40] There are a number of arguments for creating such a cabinet-level department, chief among them the traditional one that if promoting development is to be a major priority of U.S. international policies in the future, a significant agency in the federal government needs to be in place with the resources, expertise, mission, and status to pursue this goal effectively. Such a cabinet-level agency with development as its primary mission could be an effective voice for development in high-level policy discussions.

In addition, a cabinet-level department would guarantee more effective leadership. While some USAID administrators have been effective, others have come to the job ill-prepared or uninformed, leading to an erosion of the agency's morale and reputation. The importance and visibility of a new cabinet-level aid agency would encourage the president to appoint an official with the necessary knowledge of development and management skills, which, over time, would help to address some of the difficulties now hampering the most efficient delivery of foreign aid, including the excessive use of earmarks, directives, and other restrictions.[41]

Furthermore, cabinet-level development leadership is probably the only means of containing the increasing fragmentation in U.S. development activities and coordinating the disparate development programs across government. A subcabinet-level agency such as USAID or the MCC does not have the clout to take on such functions. As the government goes forward with the reorganization of both homeland security and intelligence functions, there may well be lessons for a reorganization of U.S. foreign aid administration as well. Finally, a cabinet department for development would be a powerful signal to the rest of the world that the United States is serious about addressing poverty with a peaceful and forward-looking agenda. Today, that is an especially powerful and important message for the United States.

Establish a unified aid agency within the State Department. Many of the arguments used above to create a cabinet-level organization could also be made for incorporating a unified aid agency, perhaps as a new bureau, within the Department of State. Under this scenario, such an agency would be the voice for a robust development agenda, which would clearly be perceived as an integral part of foreign policy. In the words of one former U.S. ambassador who has served in a number of developing countries:

If we are going to rationally reorganize assistance for greater impact in the post-9/11 world, we have to more clearly convey a message that says development is an integral part of our long-term national security. And people in State have to more fully integrate this message, in part by profiting from daily interaction with the perspectives of AID professionals. . . . What I have seen too frequently is host governments playing off the perception that the U.S. has two (or more) foreign policies, one led by the ambassador and the other led by the AID director. Denied by one, they cultivate the other.[42]

Arguments against folding a unified aid agency into the State Department are those cited earlier: development work is quite distinct from the core activity of the department. Development implies a long-term engagement in bringing about societal change in other countries, requiring a set of skills and a consistency over time that can prove a poor fit with the skills and more short-term time horizon and modus operandi associated with traditional diplomacy. At best, these two missions and approaches are mutually supportive. But too often they collide, as when a politically important government lacking the capacity or commitment to economic and social progress is rewarded with aid; or when aid is withdrawn from a government because of short-run diplomatic conflicts. Aid administered by USAID has, of course, been used for high-priority diplomatic purposes in the past. It would, however, be much harder for a unified aid agency located within the Department of State to resist the allocation of aid for lower priority diplomatic purposes. The exigencies of managing bilateral diplomatic relations would likely trump pursuing development in a powerful bureaucracy. Indeed, the experience of merging the U.S. Information Agency into the Department of State in the late 1990s is widely regarded (even by State Department officers) as having undercut the efficacy of U.S. public diplomacy. Mergers of agencies with different missions and asymmetric bureaucratic clout almost always create winners and losers; sadly, it is the United States that is the loser today with the evisceration of its public diplomacy muscle. Clearly, the Bush administration had similar reservations about putting development aid into the Department of State when it created a separate agency—

the Millennium Challenge Corporation—to manage the new MCA monies.

There are, of course, risks in either establishing a cabinet-level department or moving all aid programs into one department. On the one hand, a separate department, while providing greater unity in development policies and programs, might lessen the coherence of U.S. foreign policy overall; on the other, a development agency absorbed into the State Department might be undercut, compromised, or silenced. The first risk can be minimized by giving the State Department a veto over major aid programs of the Department of International Development. The second risk is much harder to protect against.

Create a unified development aid agency at the subcabinet level. A second best alternative to a cabinet-level agency is to unify aid programs (whether encompassing all major aid programs or simply those of the MCC and USAID) at the subcabinet level. This option would preserve an overall reporting relationship with the Department of State. It would incur fewer political costs but would offer fewer benefits in terms of the profile and effectiveness of development in overall U.S. policies abroad.

Programming International Assistance

If, as suggested earlier, the organization and programming systems of the U.S. government are inadequate to the task of ensuring effective and efficient development assistance programs, what is to be done? Several initiatives would seem in order:

Allow greater flexibility in strategic planning and results management. All government agencies need policies and programming systems that set out the purposes, priorities, and objectives of the agency. In international assistance, that rightly includes global, sectoral, and country-specific objectives. But these objectives should give general direction to assistance programs, allowing managers to exploit promising opportunities and to withdraw from those where success is unlikely.

Qualitative as well as quantitative indicators need to be considered. Unanticipated benefits or costs of interventions need to be identified. The time frame in which indicators are measured needs to be lengthened. Learning needs to be an important part of the results sought. In our opinion, results management should be applied realistically and for simple monitoring only—not to claim successes, to allocate resources, or to replace serious evaluation.

Tighten up and expand the evaluation function of international assistance. At least four activities need to be undertaken. First, expand evaluations to cover a larger number of aid interventions, to assess impact as well as to contribute to learning in this still experimental endeavor. Second, evaluate the success of aid interventions to achieve all of the various purposes of aid giving, in addition to improving basic socioeconomic indexes. For example, where aid is allocated primarily to expand trade, success in achieving those purposes should be part of the evaluation.

Third, make the evaluation function independent of the aid implementation agency. Evaluators need to be independent of the programs and agencies they are evaluating (but well informed with their work). They should not be individuals or organizations who depend on the aid agency for contracts. One solution is to create an evaluation service that reports both to the head of the agency and to the Office of Management and Budget.[43] It would be possible partially to staff such an agency with retiring aid professionals or to rotate aid professionals through the evaluation service as part of their career advancement, as well as to draw on those wishing to make a career in development evaluation (an expanding field) to ensure they would be well informed about aid-funded activities but without ongoing professional interests in those activities.

Finally, the findings of the evaluations must be made much more accessible, not only for aid officials but for other practitioners and the general public. During the Carter administration, the USAID administrator emphasized program evaluations, drawing staff from across the agency to conduct evaluations, having teams report directly back to him, and insisting that the evaluations be made public. At other times, though, USAID has tended to avoid publishing evaluations that were potentially critical of its work for fear of the attacks and criticisms such reporting might provoke. This is a mistake; in the long run, suppressing information can reduce the credibility of an agency and impede its learning and effectiveness.

Shift as much responsibility to recipients as they can reasonably handle, leaving the aid agency to provide a general outline of its objectives and standards. Except where the capacity is lacking, this approach would suggest a much simplified and streamlined programming process. Where recipients lack the experience or knowledge to design aid interventions, they should have access to technical assistance (provided they have the capacity to implement their aid-funded activities). The MCC envisions this approach.

Put in place a thorough review of procurement and reporting practices with a view to streamlining those processes. How effective are the very large contracts and grants that are increasingly being used in development programming? Are there really no alternatives to outsourcing the U.S. government's management responsibility for development aid? The administration should address these and other issues in the context of a thorough review of U.S. assistance. Reporting requirements on the part of aid recipients and of the aid agency itself should also be streamlined. Perhaps a new development aid agency should publish only three basic documents: a white paper outlining its main goals; a presentation of its plans for the coming year, much like the current congressional presentation; and an annual report describing its activities (including successes, failures, and lessons learned) during the previous year. Obviously, the reports demanded of an aid agency arise in part from Congress and in part from other stakeholders in the process; perhaps a newly formed aid agency could negotiate a better arrangement that would still make it fully accountable to Congress and the public but reduce the amount of time and effort demanded at present in internal and external reporting.

Examine the field-headquarters relationships in the organization of U.S. assistance efforts as well as the relationship between technical and managerial personnel. It may well be that the more nimble aid agency likely appropriate for this century will require fewer administrative staff (accounting and personnel specialists, for example) in the field (above all where countries have the capacity to manage their development aid) but more technical staff at both headquarters and in the field to quickly take advantage of emerging opportunities and adapt to shifting threats related to development.

Revisit the enabling legislation supporting U.S. international assistance. A new appropriations account structure better suited to the purposes of foreign aid in the twenty-first century would be a good place to start. Giving relevant congressional committees some shared oversight of the international portions of the domestic agencies' budgets might be difficult bureaucratically, but it would be a major step forward because it would allow, for the first time, scrutiny of the true costs and scope of international assistance.

Informing the Public about International Assistance

No transparent and accountable democratic government can operate expenditure programs year after year without a supportive public. Most countries that provide foreign aid have actively sought to inform and engage their publics in development issues and aid giving. Governments of Scandinavian countries and Japan have ensured that the school curricula include information on development; others have encouraged or even contracted with NGOs to help inform their publics on aid and development issues. The Japanese government has created a Plaza of International Cooperation in central Tokyo and organizes an annual International Cooperation Day. The Danish government sought the engagement of its business community in development activities as a way to expand knowledge of and support for development aid broadly among its citizens. In these and other countries, development education has been important, and whether as a result of these efforts or not, public support for international assistance has been commensurately high.

By contrast, the United States has done little in development education, and support for aid among the U.S. population has been among the lowest of any aid-giving country. The USAID fiscal 2005 budget for development education, for example, is a mere $750,000. More must be done in this area, not only because it is essential that Americans have a better understanding of the world in which they and their children must compete and lead, but also because this public understanding will be essential to sustain the ambitious plans for expanding international engagement to which the Bush administration is already committed. Otherwise, the debate will devolve to an "international versus domestic" budgetary tug of war, and the U.S. development agenda will likely be the loser. Given the increasing engagement in development and related issues by a wide range of private individuals and organizations, including religious agencies, the time is right to launch such an effort.

One approach could be a publicly funded foundation with a mandate to promote broad understanding of both the global issues facing the United States and especially the challenges faced by developing nations. Such a foundation might also promote student and citizen exchanges, language competence and cultural literacy, and research and training programs to build a new generation of internationally knowledgeable Americans. Last, if any new development aid agency is established, public awareness should be among its highest priorities.

Conclusion

The opportunities to reduce the burden of poverty and disease and to integrate even the poorest countries into the international community have never been greater. The consequences of neglecting to do so have, at the same time, never been more obvious. The United States has begun to respond to these new realities both by recognizing international development as critical to U.S. foreign policy and security and by boosting foreign aid levels more rapidly than at any time since the 1960s. But the organization, structure, and processes of U.S. aid giving today are simply not well suited to the challenges and opportunities before us. We cannot afford to squander precious time and resources by continuing to tolerate the cumbersome processes and unclear or overlapping mandates of the myriad government agencies now engaged in foreign aid. It is time for a change.

Notes

1. White House, "Introduction," *The National Security Strategy of the United States,* September 2002 (www.whitehouse.gov/nsc/nss.html).

2. Program on International Policy Attitudes, *Americans on Foreign Aid and World Hunger: A Study of U.S. Public Attitudes,* University of Maryland, February 2, 2001 (www.pipa.org/OnlineReports/BFW/finding1.html).

3. Development Assistance Committee, Organization for Economic Cooperation and Development, *International Development Statistics* (www.oecd.org/dataoecd/50/17/5037721.htm). The level went from $2.1 billion to $4.2 billion. The data do not include government aid channeled through NGOs.

4. See Foundation Center, *International Grantmaking III* (http://fdncenter.org/research/trends_analysis/pdf/intlhlts.pdf).

5. Amartya Sen, *Development as Freedom* (New York: Anchor Books, 1999).

6. The Development Assistance Committee (DAC) of the Organization for Economic Cooperation and Development (OECD) is the principal body through which thirty donor countries deal collectively with issues related to cooperation with developing countries.

7. Development Assistance Committee, *International Development Statistics.*

8. These data are drawn from different sources but are roughly comparable. Data on the total amount of U.S. aid since 1946 are from USAID, *U.S. Overseas Loans and Grants* (the "Greenbook") (http://qesdb.cdie.org/gbk/). State Department funds are disbursements or estimated disbursements. They include aid to poor, middle-, and upper-income developing countries. They are not net of repayments, which is very small in any case. U.S. aid data from the Greenbook are mainly obligations and do not net out repayments. All of these data are in current dollars.

9. All these funds, with the exception of the cash transfer to Israel, are applied to specific development activities within the recipient country.

10. Development Assistance Committee, *Review of the Development Co-operation Policies and Programmes of the United States* (Paris: OECD, 2002), p. 8.

11. Overseas Presence Advisory Panel, *America's Overseas Presence in the 21st Century* (Washington: State Department, November 1999), p. 16.

12. For one effort to estimate some of these expenditures, see Benjamin Nelson, "International Affairs: Activities of Domestic Agencies," Testimony before the Task Force on International Affairs, Committee on the Budget, U.S. Senate (Washington: U.S. General Accounting Office, GAO/T-NSIAD-98-174, June 4, 1998). See also the National Security Council, PRD-20, "International Activities of U.S. Government Agencies," photocopy. This is an unpublished, unclassified assessment by the Office of Management and Budget, undertaken in 1993, of all international activities of U.S. government agencies, including actual data for 1992, estimated data for 1993, and proposed data for 1994. It differentiates between USAID-funded activities by other government agencies and activities funded from the appropriations for those agencies. Gathering the data involved consulting with each agency's budget office individually.

13. Overseas Presence Advisory Panel, p. 64.

14. Ibid.

15. To our knowledge, thus far no effort has been made to identify the different diplomatic (international security or political) goals that U.S. foreign aid is meant to achieve and to assess the effectiveness of aid in furthering those goals. Admittedly not an easy task, a study needs to be undertaken given the use of aid for these purposes and the importance of demonstrating results.

16. Personal correspondence with J. Brian Atwood, January 3, 2005.

17. See www.usaid.gov/about_usaid/usaidhist.html.

18. USAID's personnel structure has several categories: direct-hire foreign service personnel, who are full-time professionals serving both in Washington and overseas; and direct-hire civil servants who are also full-time professionals who serve primarily in Washington. To supplement these staffs (which are often capped at particular levels by the Office of Management and Budget and Congress), USAID hires personal service contractors (PSCs)—individuals, usually with particular expertise, who serve as contractors for a specified period (though these periods are often extended so that it is sometimes diffi-

cult to distinguish direct-hire staff from PSCs). Finally, there are foreign service nationals—professionals (often extremely highly skilled and effective) hired in the recipient country to provide functions needed by USAID's field missions.

Within the program and budgetary constraints imposed by headquarters, based on administration and congressional decisions, field mission directors can decide on the details of aid-funded activities, commit directly up to $5 million in aid expenditures on these activities, and select organizations to implement them (usually as a result of a competitive bidding process).

19. USAID's field missions already exhibit considerable diversity in their structures. Some are "traditional" with a number of professional staff. Some are staffed with only one or two professionals to oversee activities. Some are in a "wheel and spoke" arrangement, with a central mission providing needed services to much smaller missions in nearby countries. Some are "regional platforms," providing functional services to field missions in the region. See, for example, David Eckerson, Rose Marie Depp, and others, *USAID Overseas Workforce*, Operations Paper 1 (Washington: USAID, 2003).

20. Judith Tendler, *Inside International Assistance* (Johns Hopkins University Press, 1975).

21. See Cynthia Clapp-Wincek and Richard Blue, "Evaluation of Recent USAID Evaluation Experience," Special Evaluation, PN-ACG-632, Working Paper 320 (USAID, Center for Development Information and Evaluation, 2001) (www.dec.org/search/dexs/index.cfm?fuseaction=docsresults.dexs& cfid=62594&cftoken=96191714).

22. For polls on U.S. attitudes toward international assistance, see Chicago Council on Foreign Relations, "Worldviews 2002" (www. worldviews.org/detailreports/usreport.pdf). The Chicago Council has conducted polls of U.S. attitudes toward international assistance and other programs over a number of years. They show a positive support for aid by the public but at lower levels than polls with comparable questions show for most of Europe. See also the Program on International Public Attitudes, "Americans on International Assistance and World Hunger," 2001 (www. pipa.org/OnlineReports/BFW/finding1.html).

23. At the time of this writing, no mention of "development education" appears on the USAID website. In the early Clinton administration, a few million dollars were dedicated to this purpose, used in part to help educate librarians on where to find information. Later, USAID organized some innovative

conferences in various parts of the United States, called "Lessons without Borders," to discuss issues and solutions relevant both at home and abroad—for example, literacy education. But these were not continued in the Bush administration.

24. *The Congressional Globe*, 29 Cong. 2 sess., U.S. Senate, p. 512. From "U.S. Congressional Documents and Debates 1774–1873," *American Memory*, Library of Congress.

25. Ibid., p. 534.

26. There is no rating system to our knowledge that would measure the overall effectiveness of aid agencies. Frequent queries to aid officials both in the United States and abroad as to which agencies perform the best typically elicit groups of agencies rather than a listing according to performance. DFID, USAID, aid agencies in Germany and Denmark, and those in other Nordic countries are often mentioned as being among the better performers in this rather unsystematic exercise.

27. For more details on the way aid is and can be organized, see Hyun-sih Chang, Arthur Fell, and Michael Lang, *A Comparison of Management Systems for Development Cooperation in OECD/DAC Countries* (Paris: OECD, 1999) (www.oecd.org/dataoecd/40/28/2094873.pdf).

28. See A. Binnendijk, *Results-Based Management in Donor Agencies*, DAC Working Party on Aid Evaluation (Paris: OECD, 2001) (www.oecd.org/dataoecd/16/25/1886519.pdf).

29. For more on the approach to aid delivery in this latter organization, see Steve Radelet, *The Global Fund to Fight AIDS, Tuberculosis, and Malaria: Progress, Potential, and Challenges for the Future* (Washington: Center for Global Development, June 2004).

30. Foundation Center, *International Grantmaking III*, p. 2.

31. For an assessment of the potential purchasing power among the poor for the products of international private enterprises, see C. K. Prahalad, *The Fortune at the Bottom of the Pyramid: Eradicating Poverty through Profits* (Saddle River, N.J.: Wharton School Publishing, 2005).

32. For example, the Center for Global Development—the principal research institute in Washington, D.C., focused on development issues, was established with a generous grant from one such individual—Ed Scott, cofounder of BAE Systems, an Internet company.

33. See the Inter-American Development Bank website (www.iadb.org/exr/remittances/index.cfm?Language=English).

34. While the exact amount of remittances available for investment is unknown, this is the estimate provided by Ernesto Armenteros, president,

Grupo Quisqueyana, at a Center for Global Development panel discussion on remittances, October 12, 2004.

35. See Federal Reserve Bank of Dallas, "Workers Remittances to Mexico," *Business Frontier*, issue 1, El Paso, 2004, pp. 3–4 (www.dallasfed.org/research/busfront/bus0401.pdf).

36. See http://koica.go.kr/.

37. For more on the challenges of weak and failing states, see Jeremy Weinstein, John Edward Porter, and Stuart Eizenstat, *On the Brink: Weak States and U.S. National Security, A Report of the Commission for Weak States and U.S. National Security* (Washington: Center for Global Development, 2004) (www.cgdev.org/docs/Full_Report.pdf).

38. This term comes from the telecommunications industry and refers to the number of entities sending and receiving communications in a particular system.

39. While a case could be made for also folding the Peace Corps into a U.S. government aid agency, the benefit is arguable. The Peace Corps acts almost like an NGO by training volunteers who work abroad—making it a retailer rather than a wholesaler. Further, the Peace Corps, and its volunteers, has for the most part been shielded from controversial elements of U.S. foreign policy because of its independent status.

40. Weinstein, Porter, and Eizenstat, *On the Brink*.

41. Because it does not have strong domestic support and has borne problems of leadership, foreign aid has been especially vulnerable to externally and internally imposed restrictions and limitations, well beyond those required for public accountability. The restrictions, in turn, lead to a lack of coherence and innovation in the aid program, potentially reducing its effectiveness and generating public criticisms that can lead to yet further restrictions.

42. Ambassador Peter Chaveas (former U.S. ambassador to Malawi), personal correspondence, December 2004.

43. The World Bank recognized the importance of independence of such evaluators by creating the Operations Evaluation Department, which reports to the bank's executive directors as well as its own department director.

Index